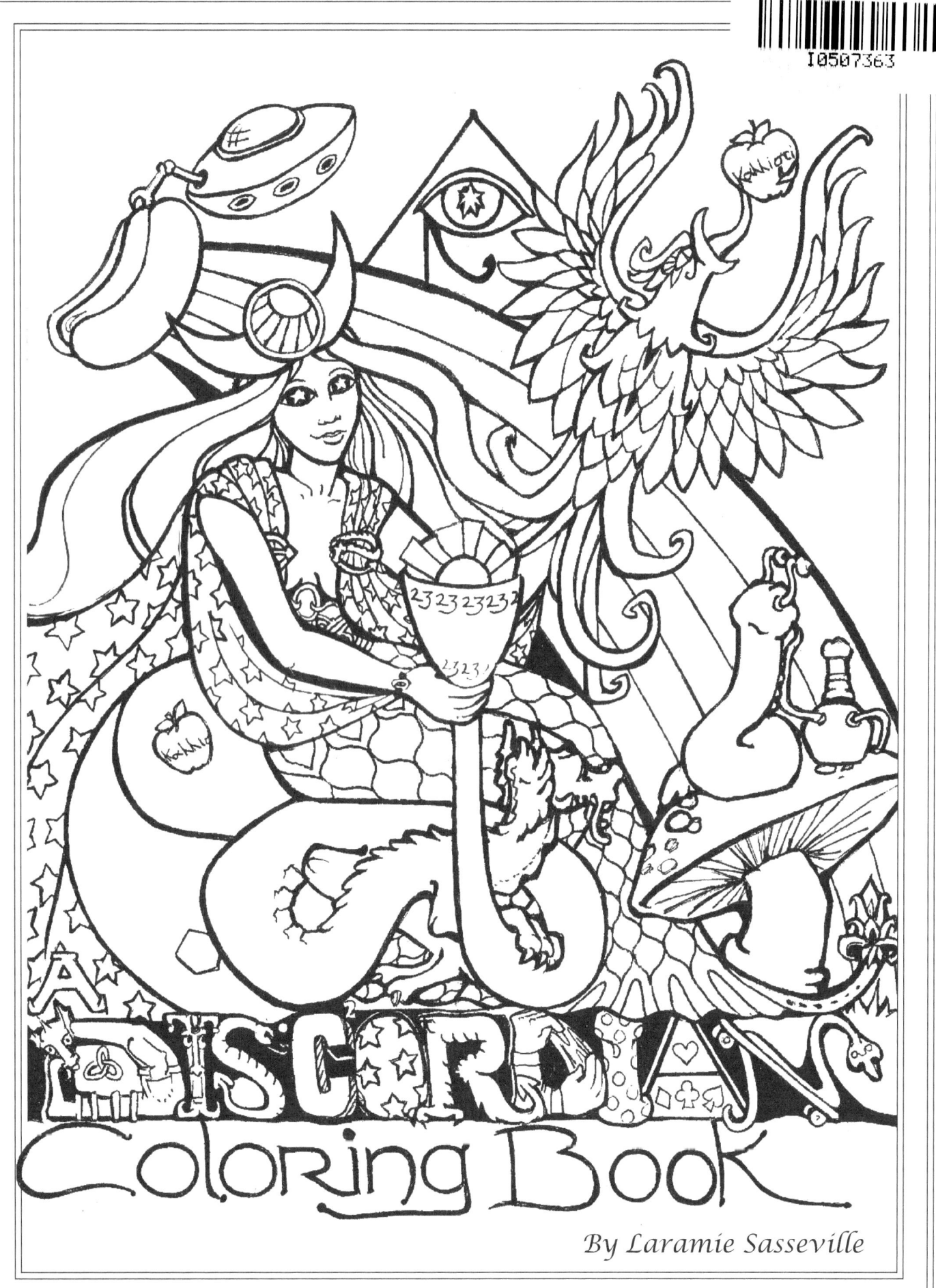

At this time of producing the 3ⁿᵈ edition of "A Discordian Coloring Book" it is the Year 2015. Never has the random principle of Eris been more evident in the world, and never have we been more in need of appealing to her in a spirit of light-heartedness and fun. Let us all remember the Holy Chao and leaven the orderly with playfulness and lighten our disorderly impulses with a sense of humane bounds.

This edition is dedicated to all those friends who keep the faith:

Jill Boughner, Sam Nygren, Rosalind Nelson, Mary Anne Beers, Thorin Tatge, Richard Tatge, Carolyn Brust, Nate Bucklin, Ray Kivlahan, Cecilia Henle, Marty Hiller, Rich Brown, Sharon Kahn, Karen Horner, The 2ⁿᵈ Sunday Rise Up Singing group, all the residents of The Courts of Chaos, Mnstf, MiniCon, the 4ᵗʰ Saturday Filkers, The Friday Gamesday Players, Andy Anda, Bonnie and Chas Somdahl, Becca Allen, ProDea and all my LJ Friends.

- Laramie Sasseville

Copyright 1982 by Laramie Sasseville

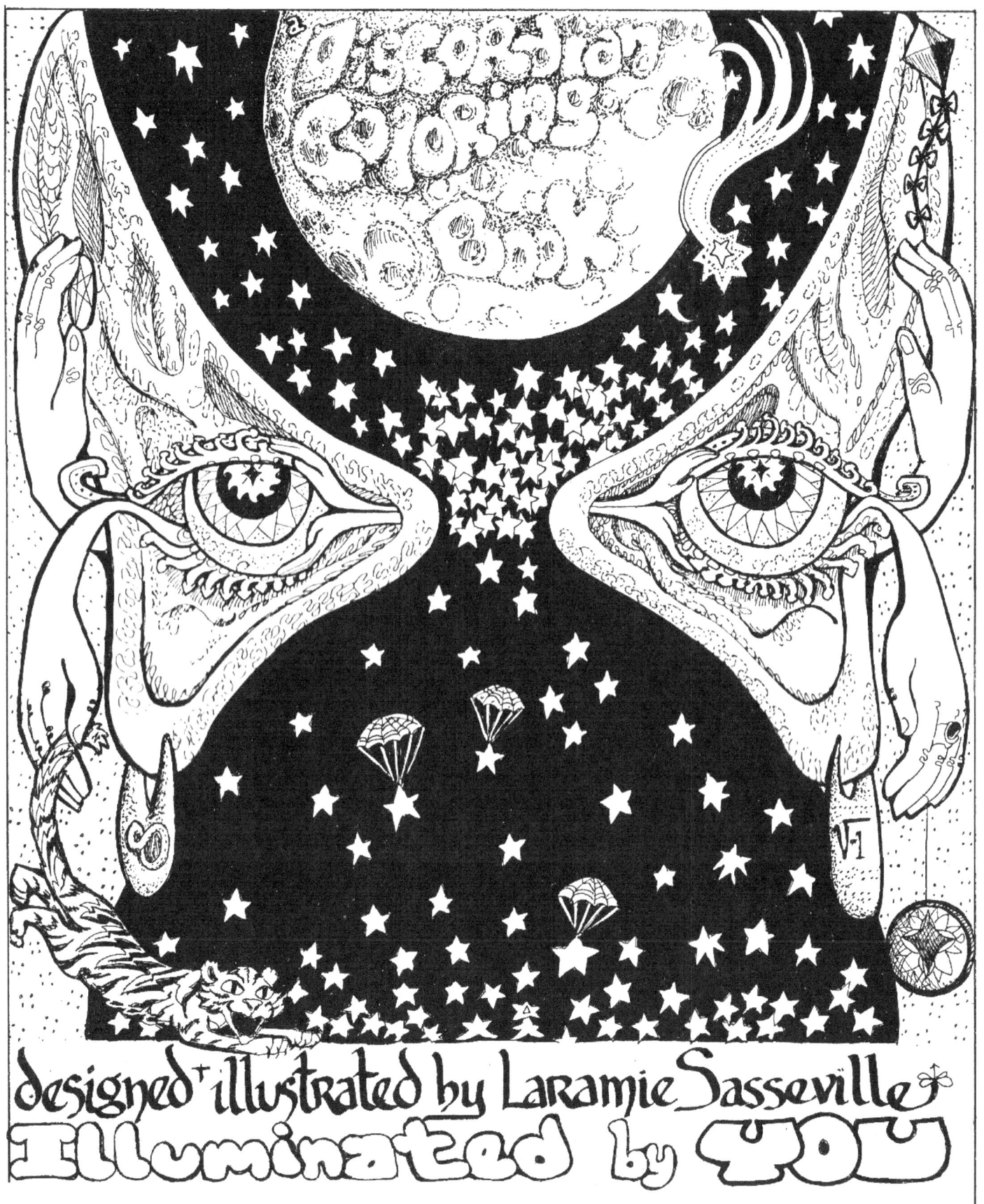

Inspired by 'The Principia Discordia' of Malaclypse the Younger, the 'Illuminatus' trilogy by Robert Shea and Robert Anton Wilson, and the accumulated wisdom of the ages.

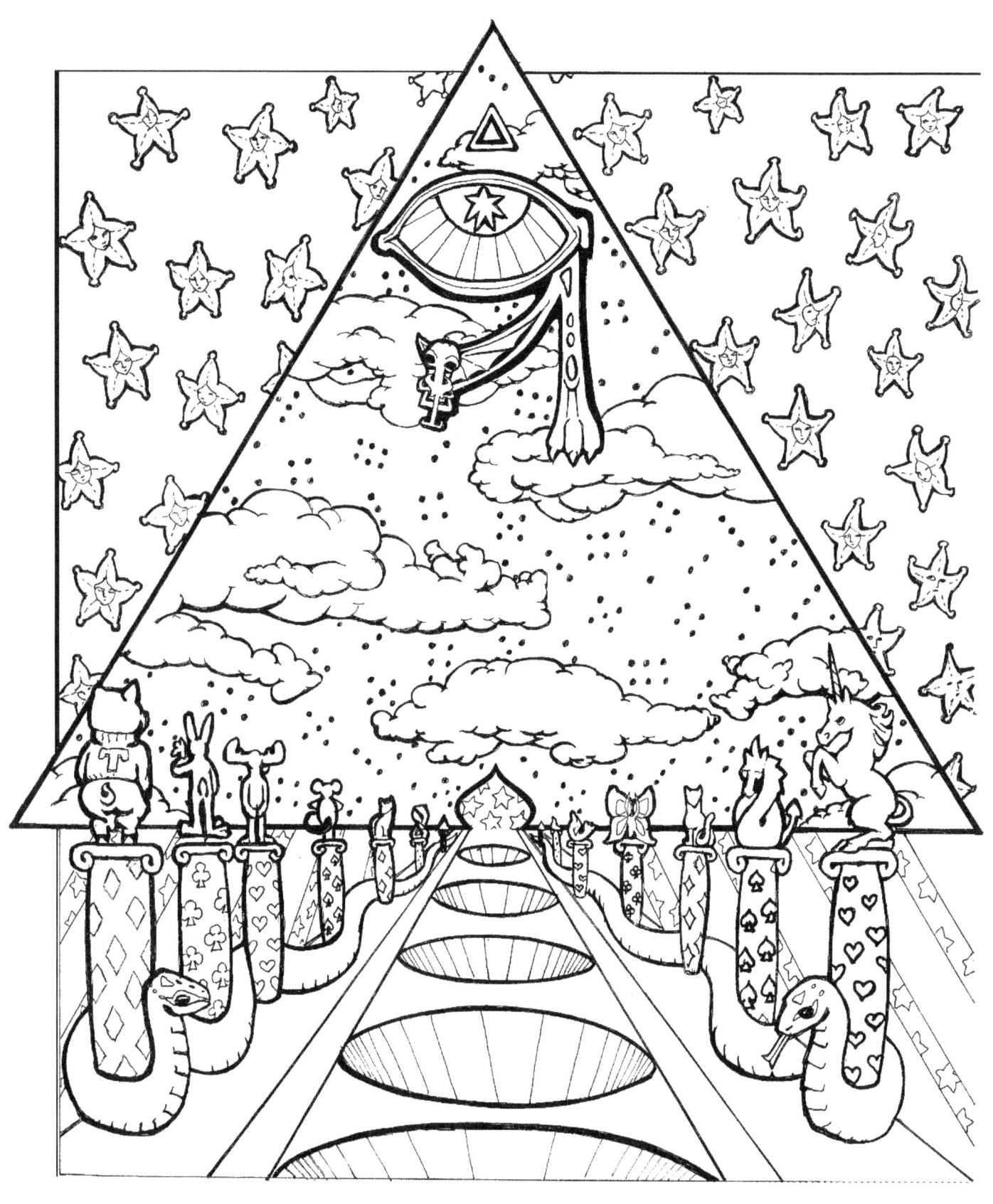

Everything is in some sense true, in some sense false and in some sense meaningless..."

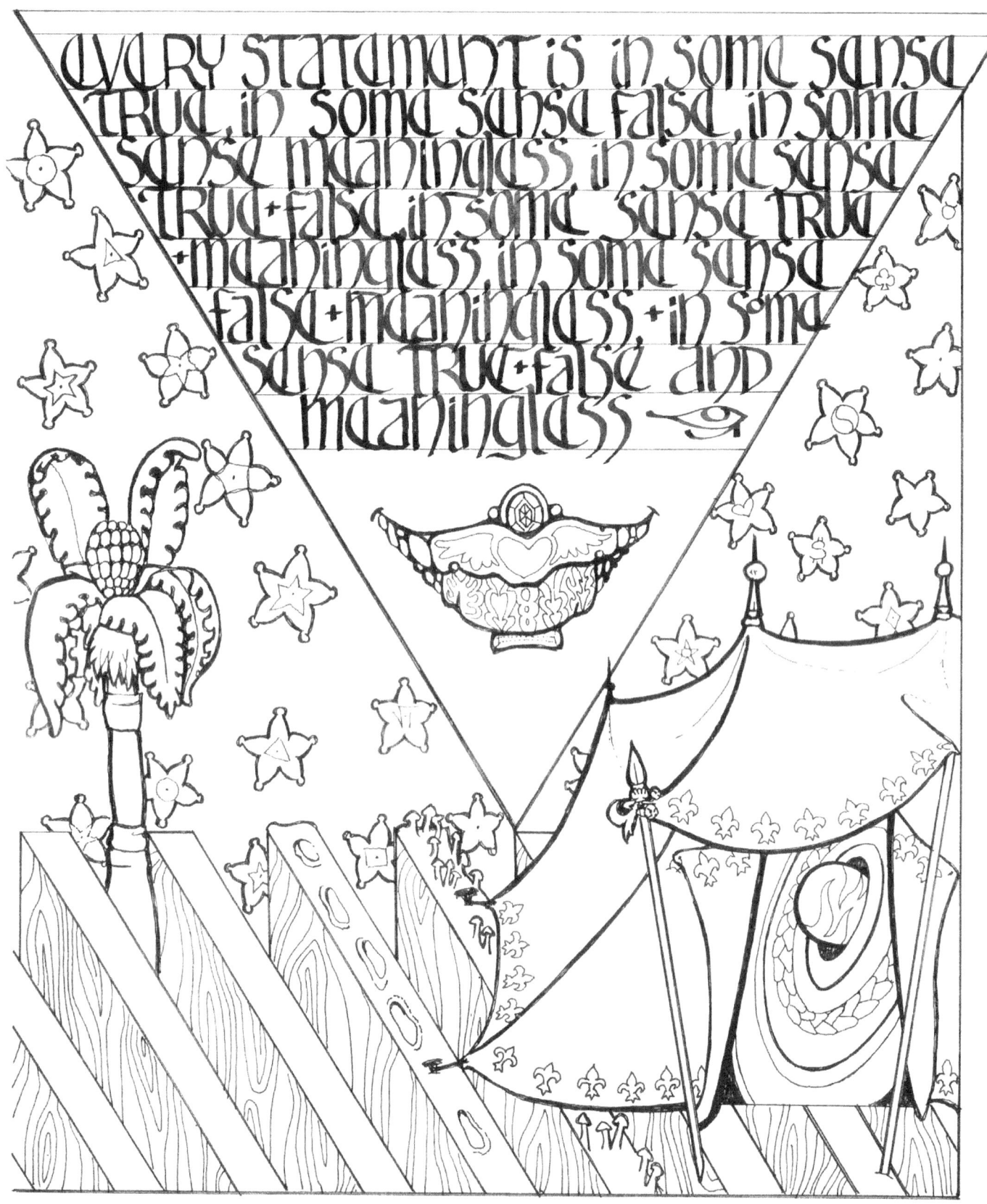

In some sense true and false, in some sense true and meaningless, in some sense false and meaningless, and in some sense true and false and meaningless."

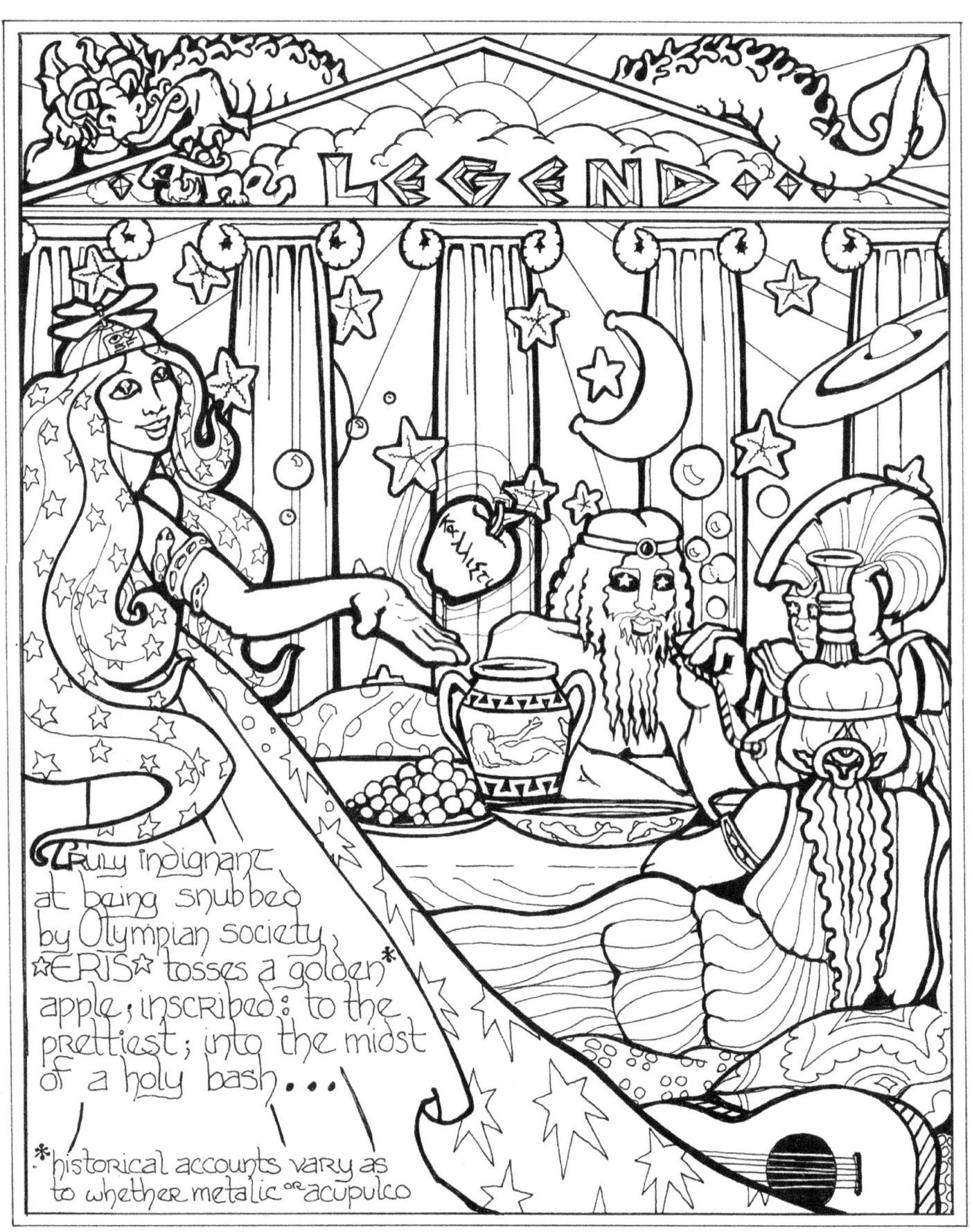

Truly indignant at being snubbed by Olympian society, Eris tosses a golden apple inscribed, "To the Prettiest," into the midst of a holy bash...

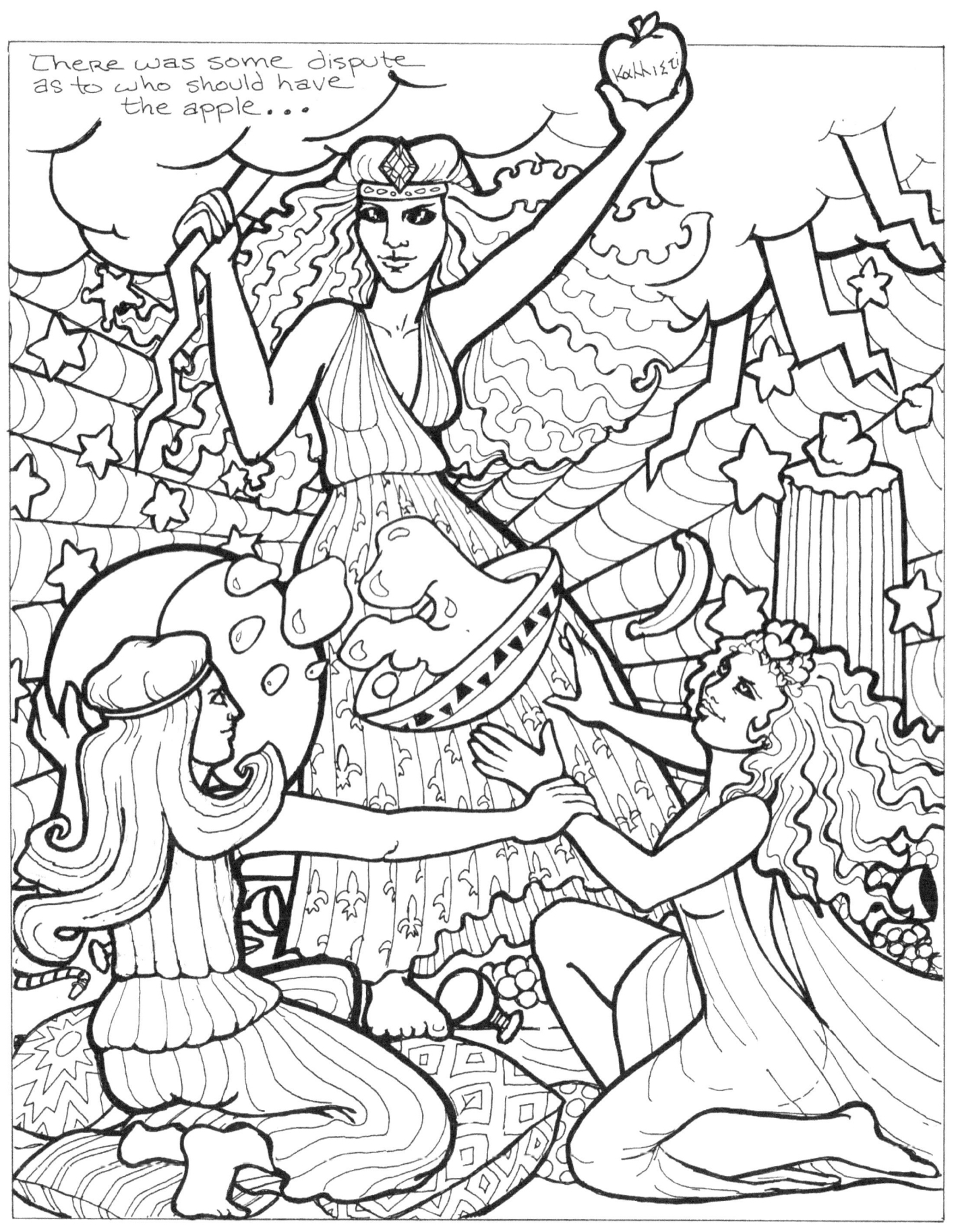

There was some dispute as to who should have the apple...

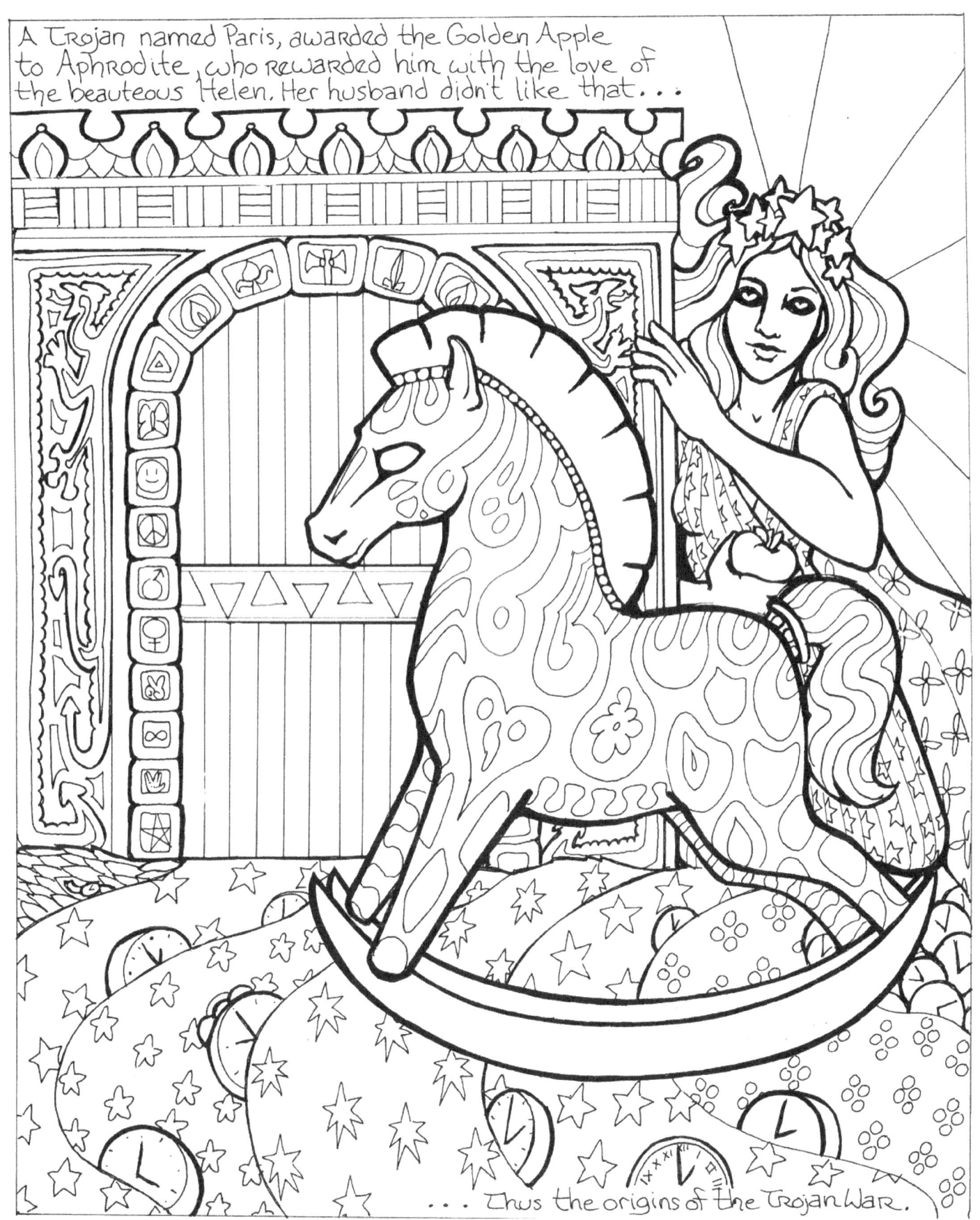

A Trojan named Paris awarded the Golden Apple to Aphrodite, who rewarded him with the love of the beauteous Helen. Her husband didn't like that...

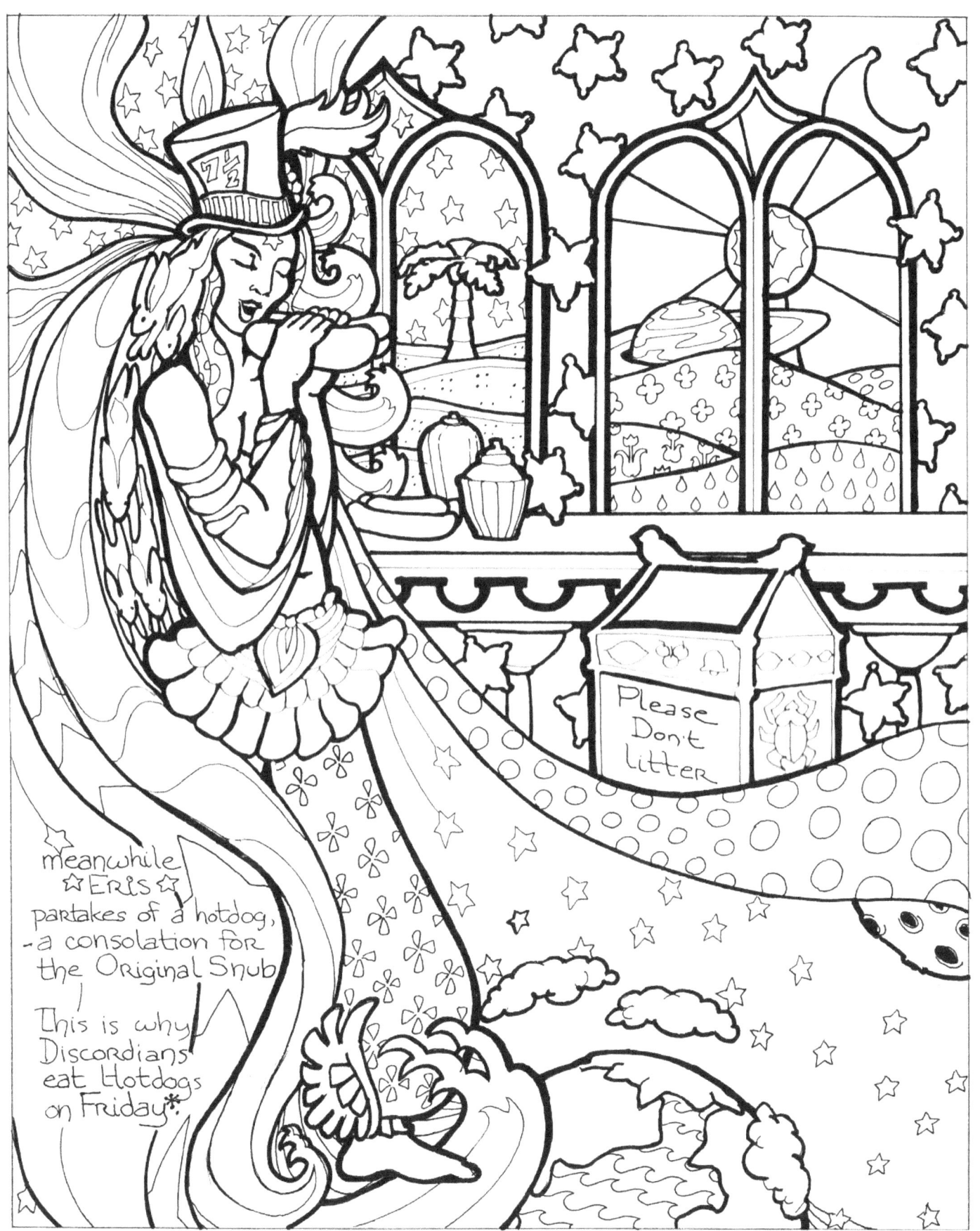

* *A remonstrance against Catholic Christiandom (no meat on Friday), Judaism (no meat of Pork), Hindic peoples (no meat of Beef), Buddhists (no meat of animals) and Discordians (no hotdog buns.)*

The Revelation:

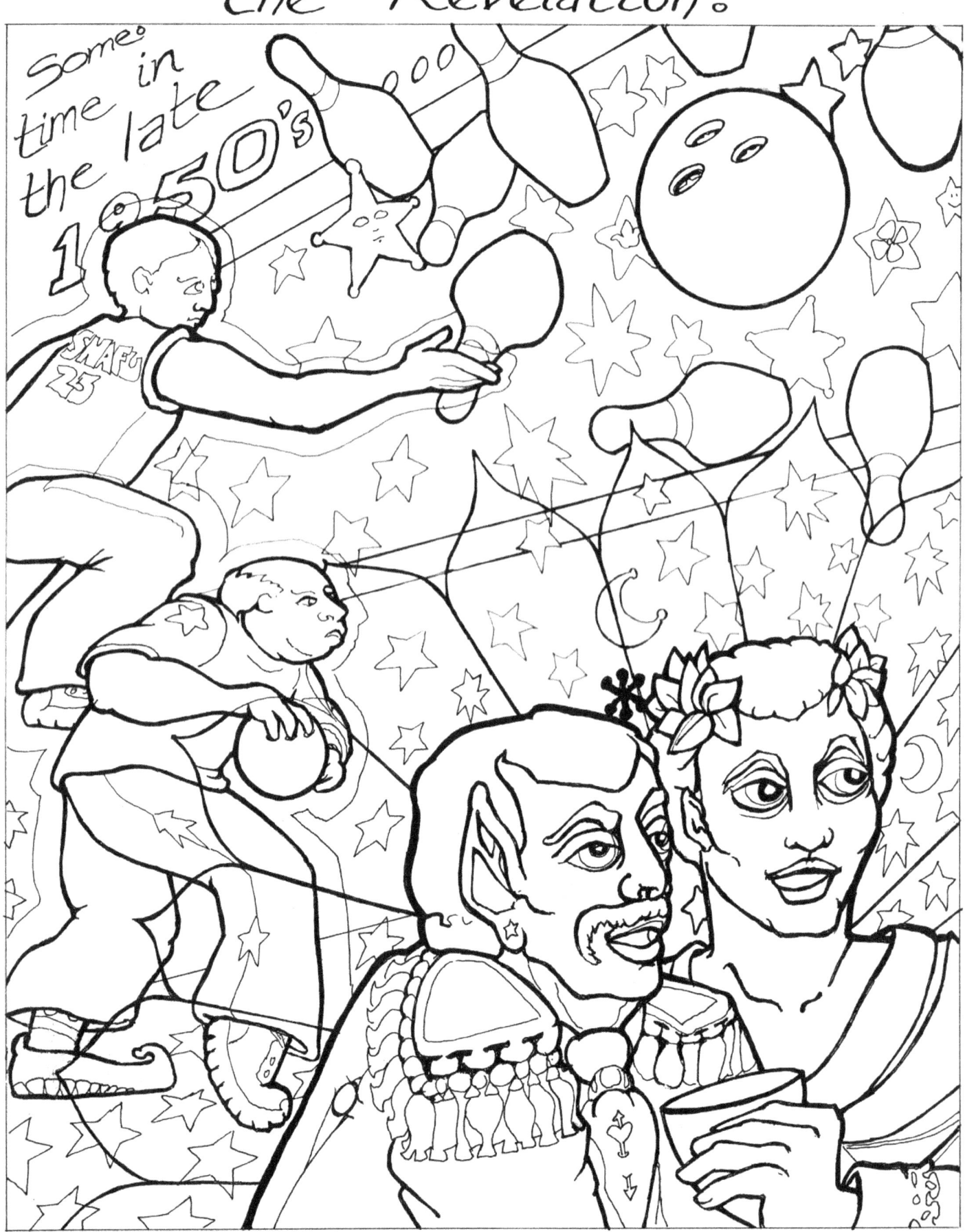

*Omar Ravenhurst and Malaclypse the Younger

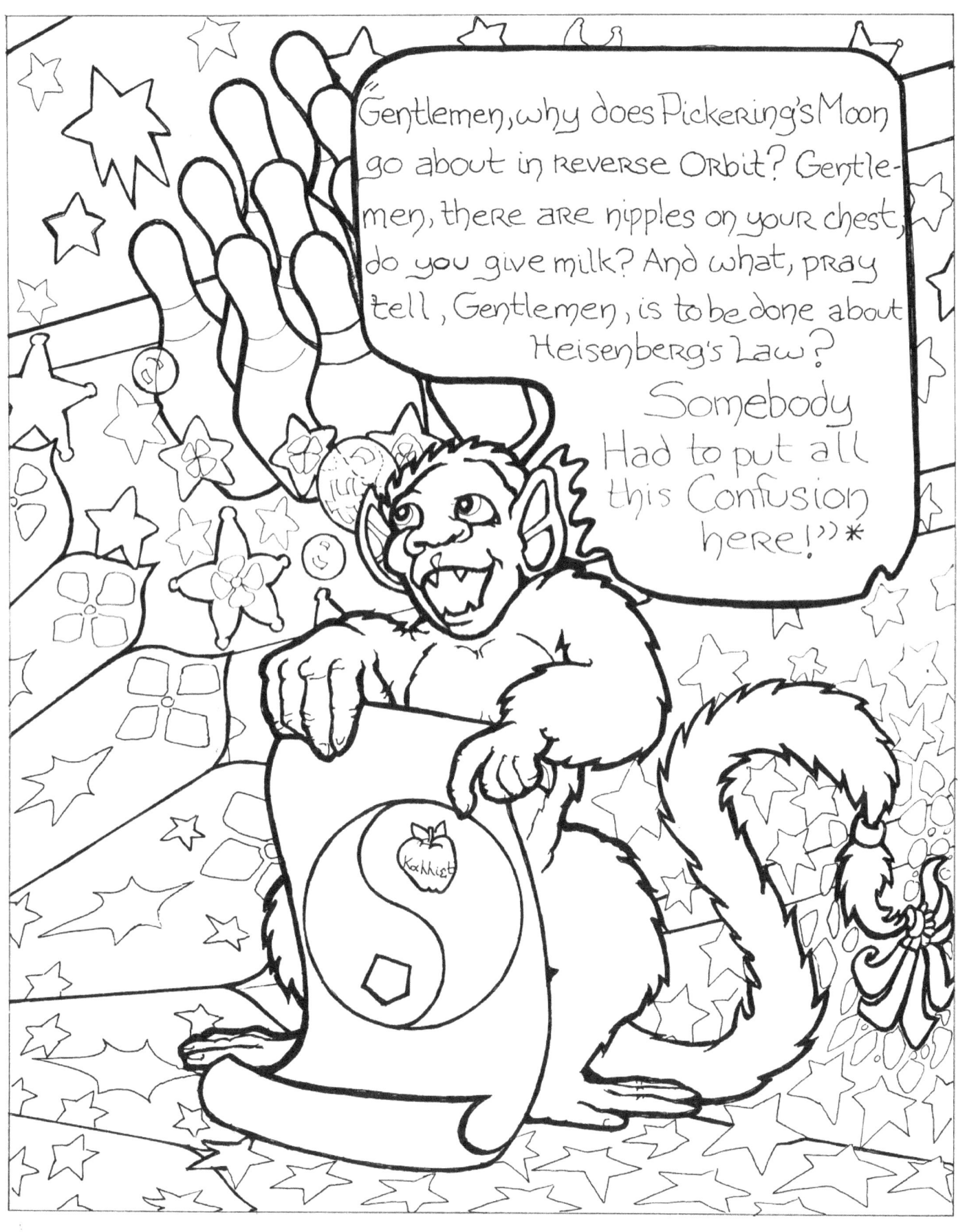

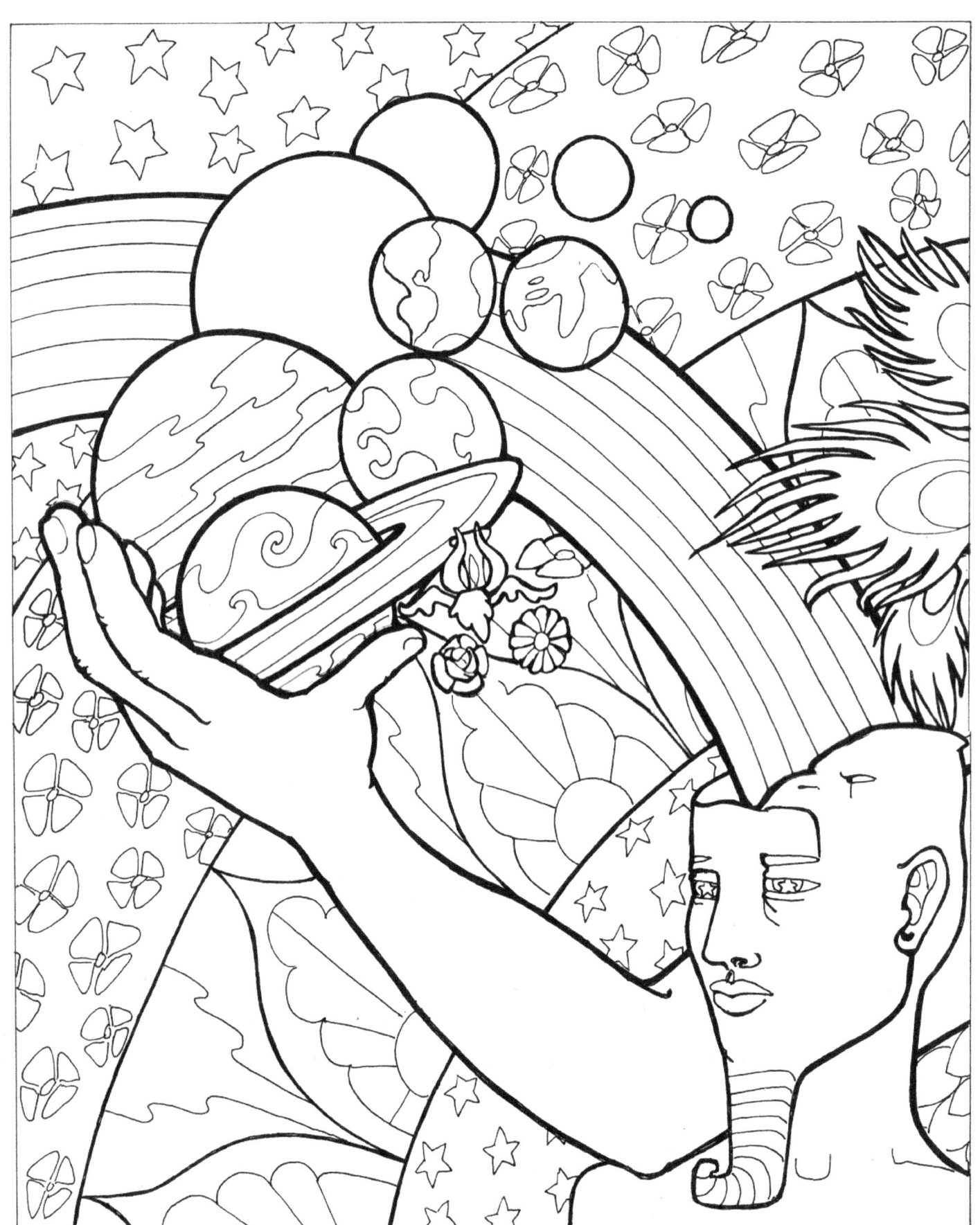

I am chaos. I am the substance from which your artists and scientists build rhythms. I am the spirit with which your children and clowns laugh in happy anarchy.

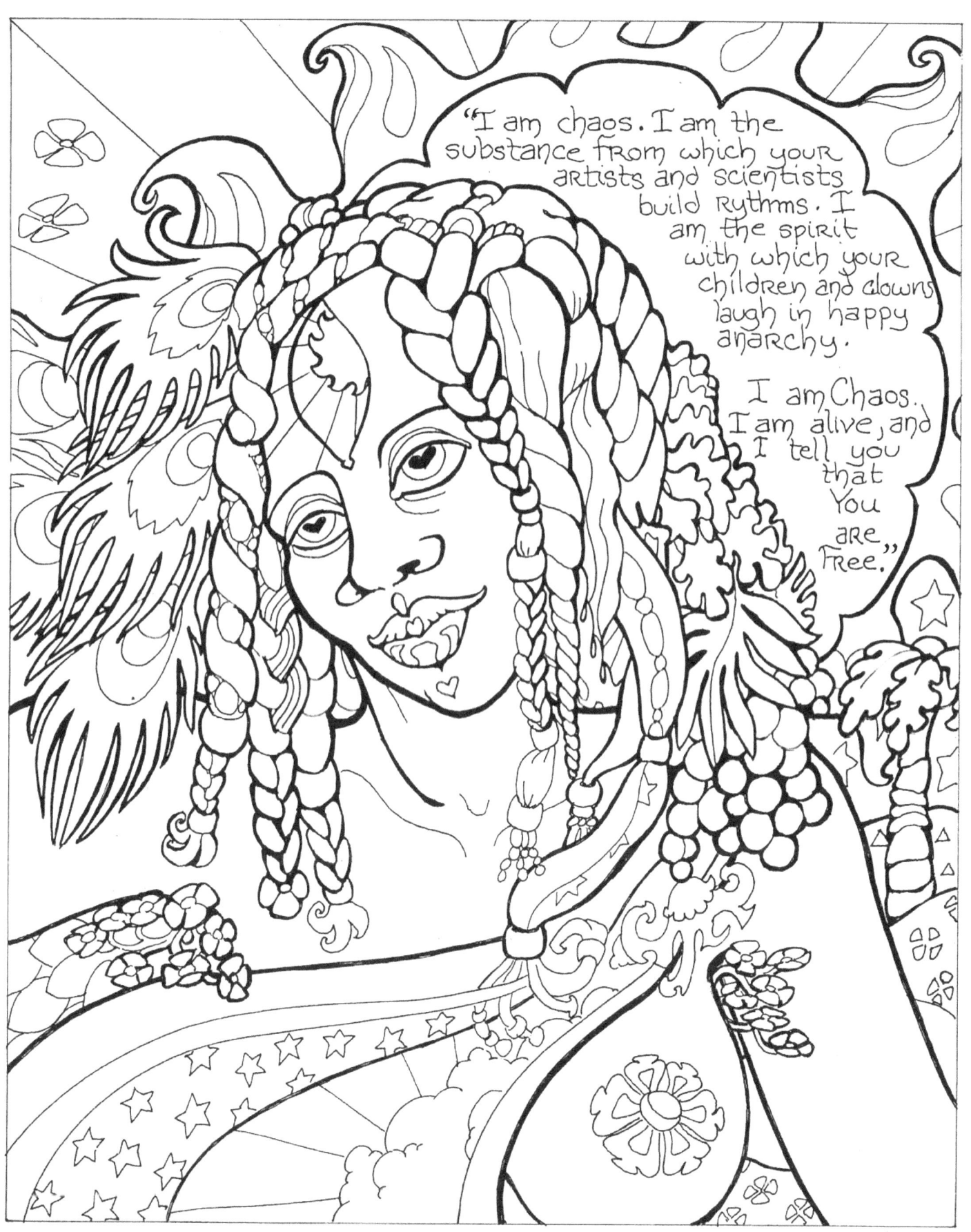

"I am Chaos. I am alive, and I tell you that you are free."

Discordian Catma,

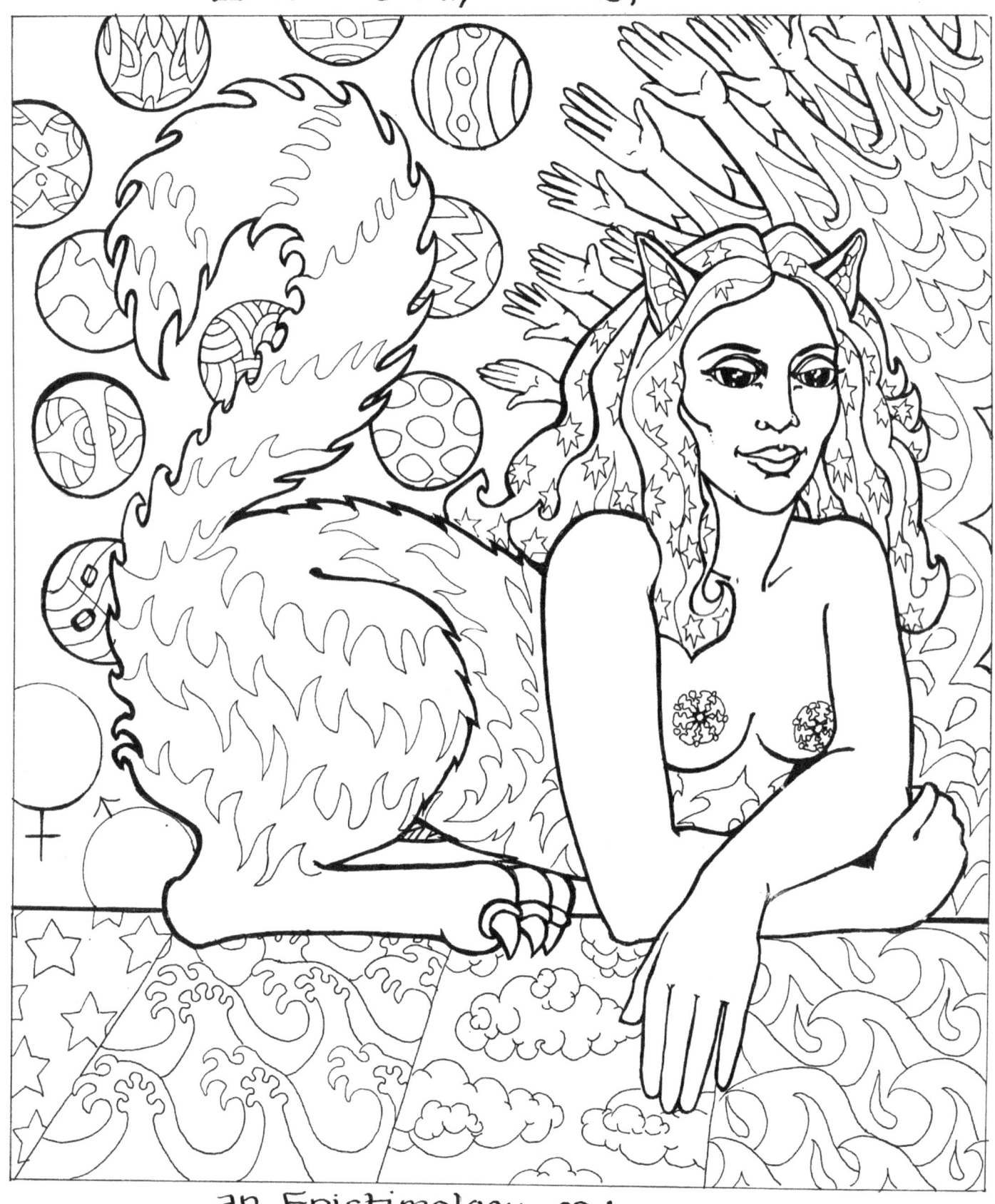

an Epistimology, or:

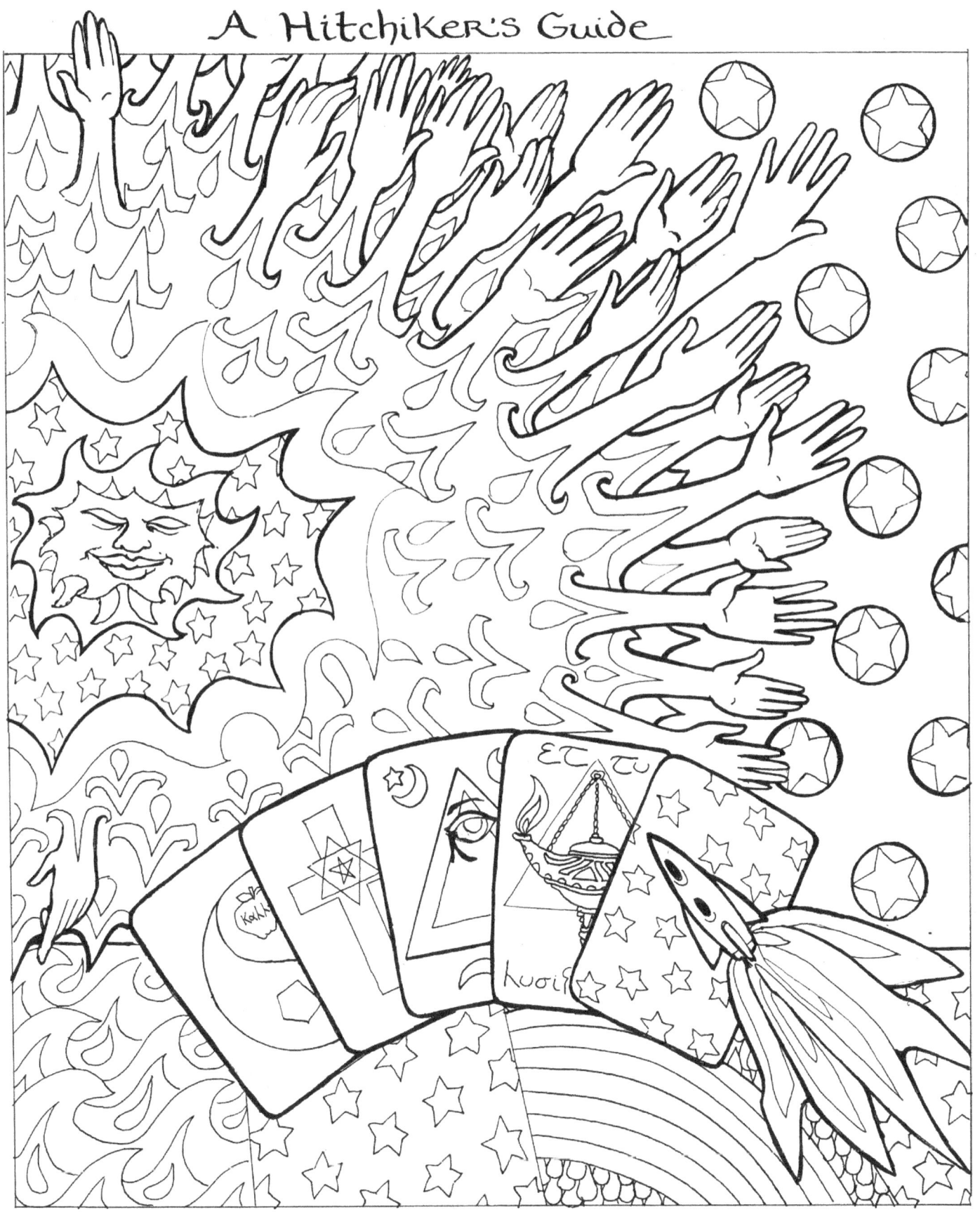

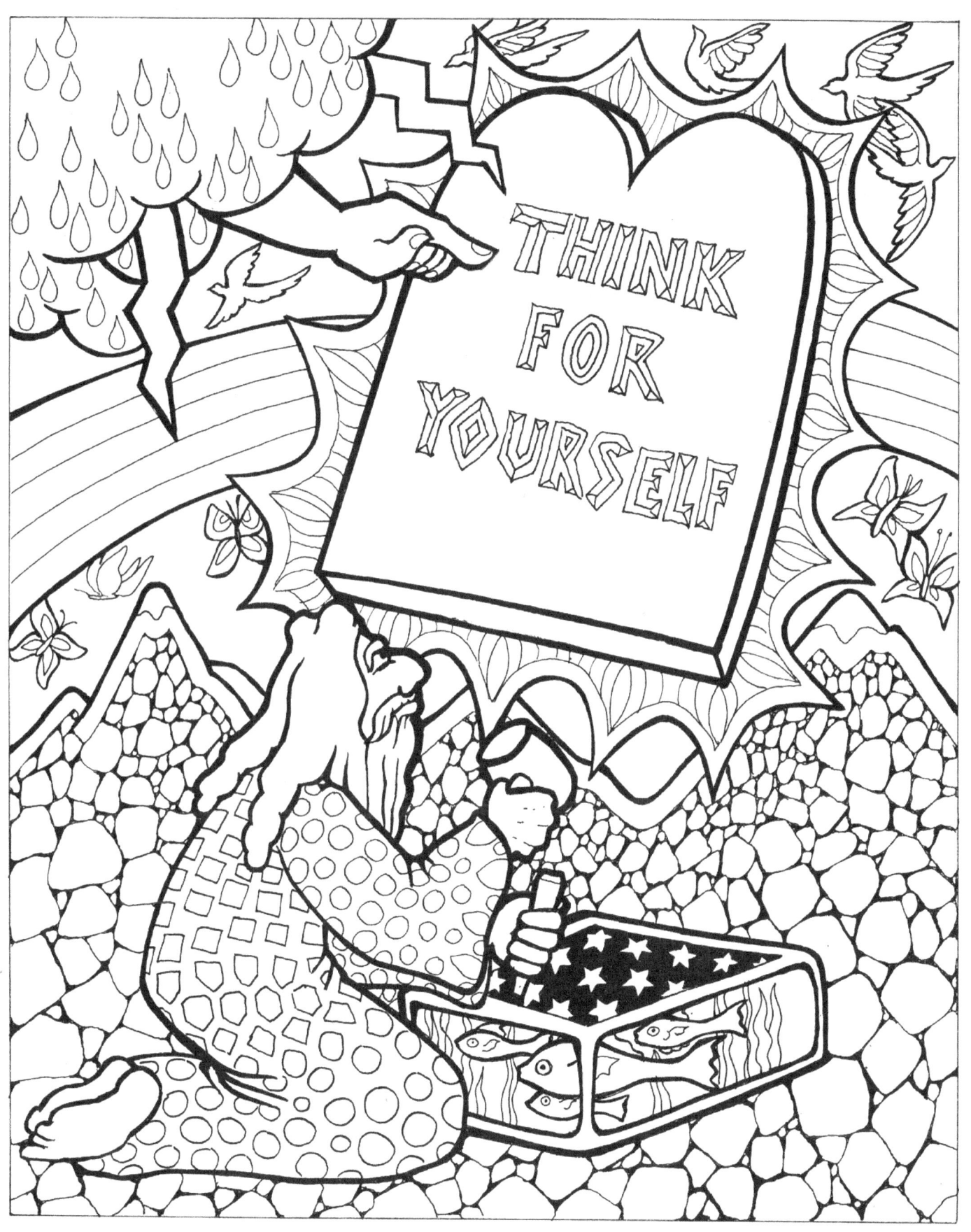

Convictions Cause Convicts

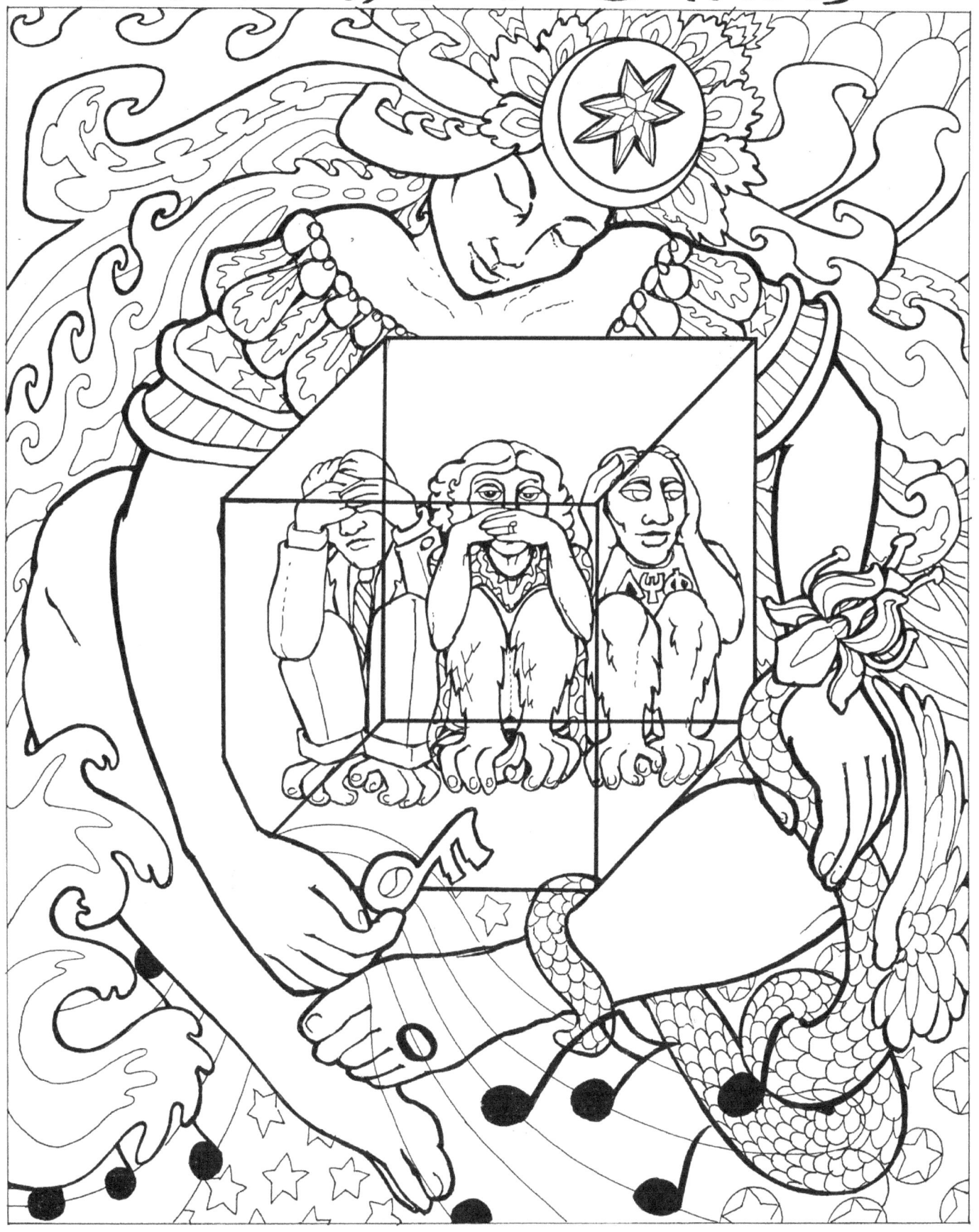

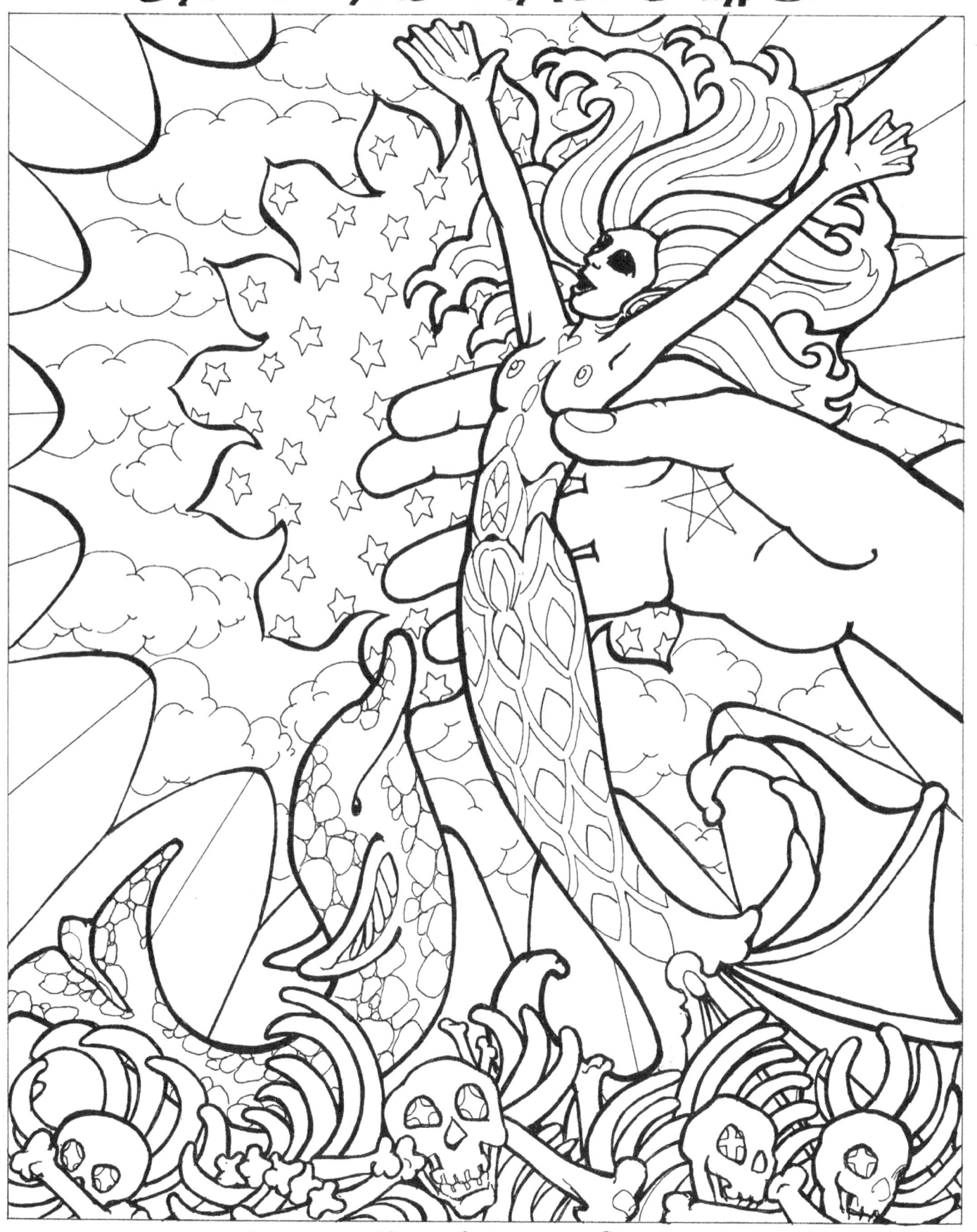

The Pun is Mighter

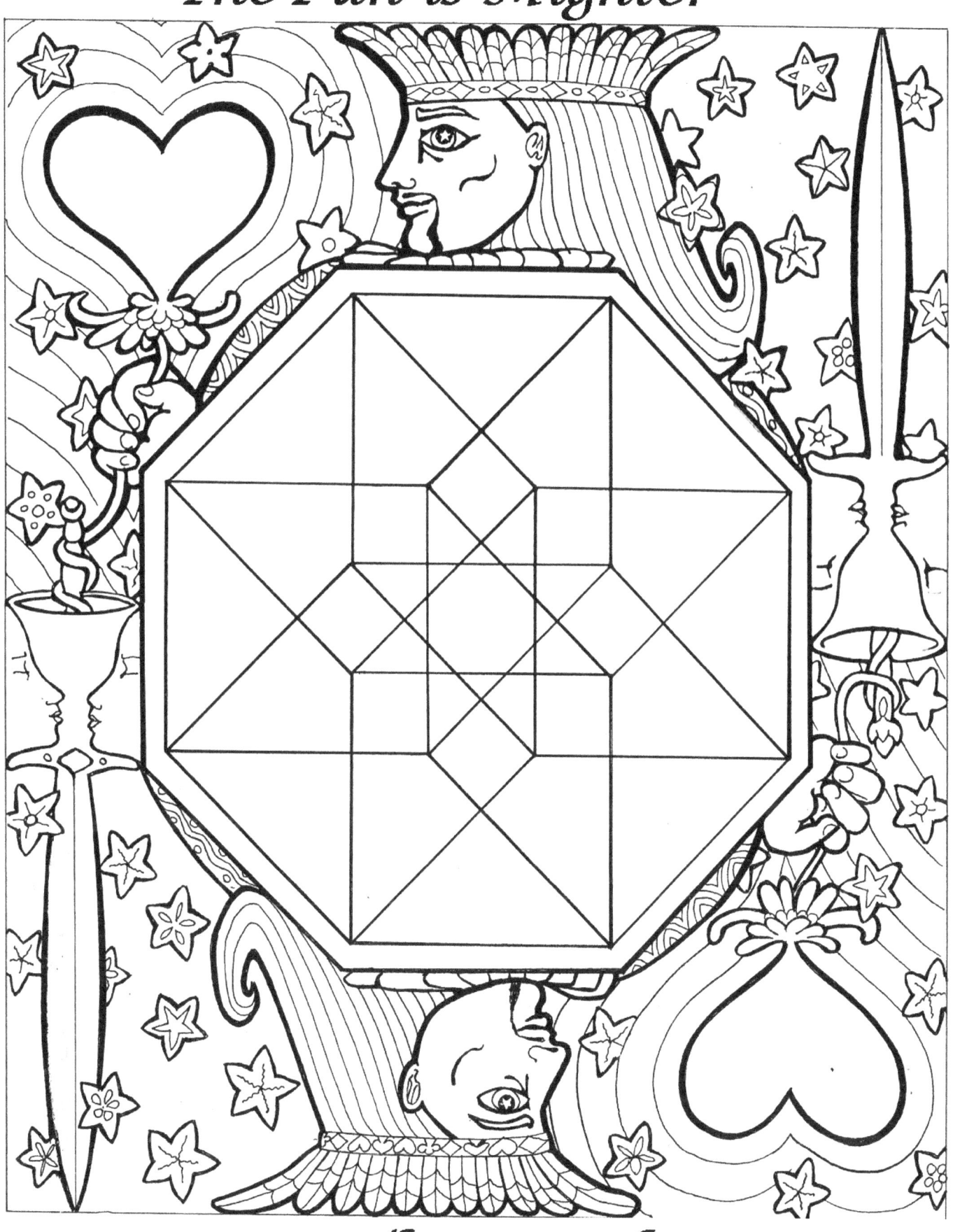

The Sword
-Hagbard Celine

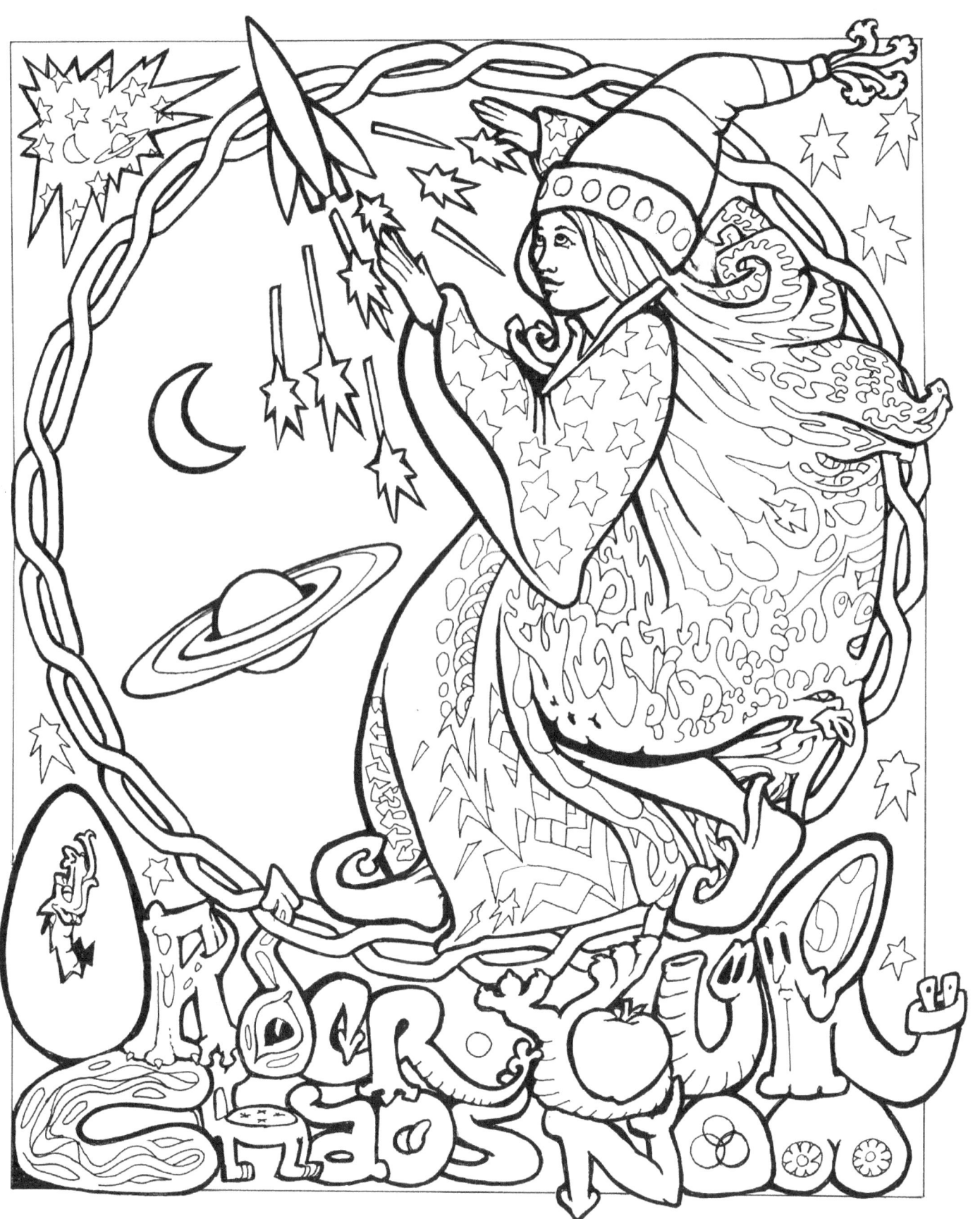

Order Your Chaos Now

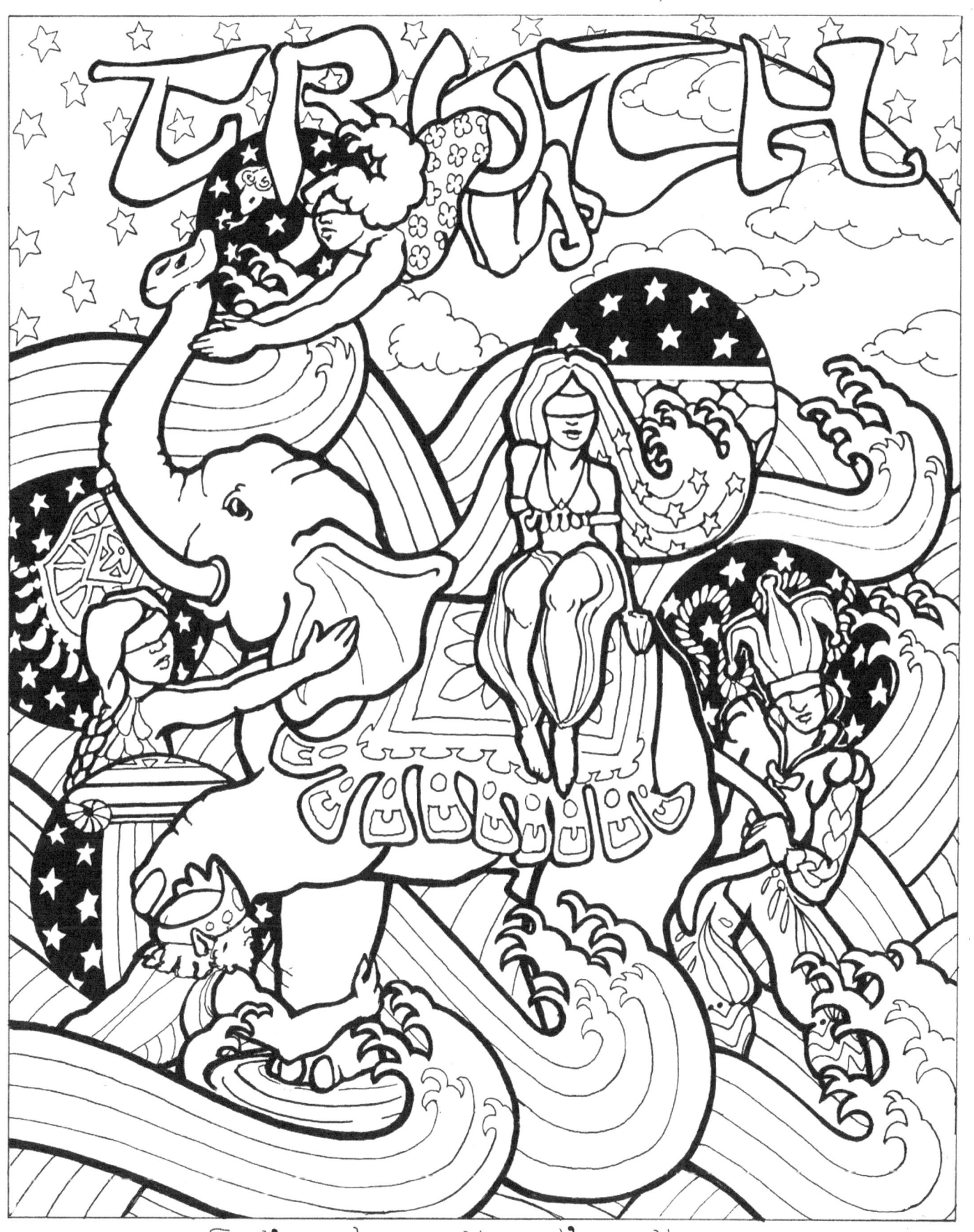

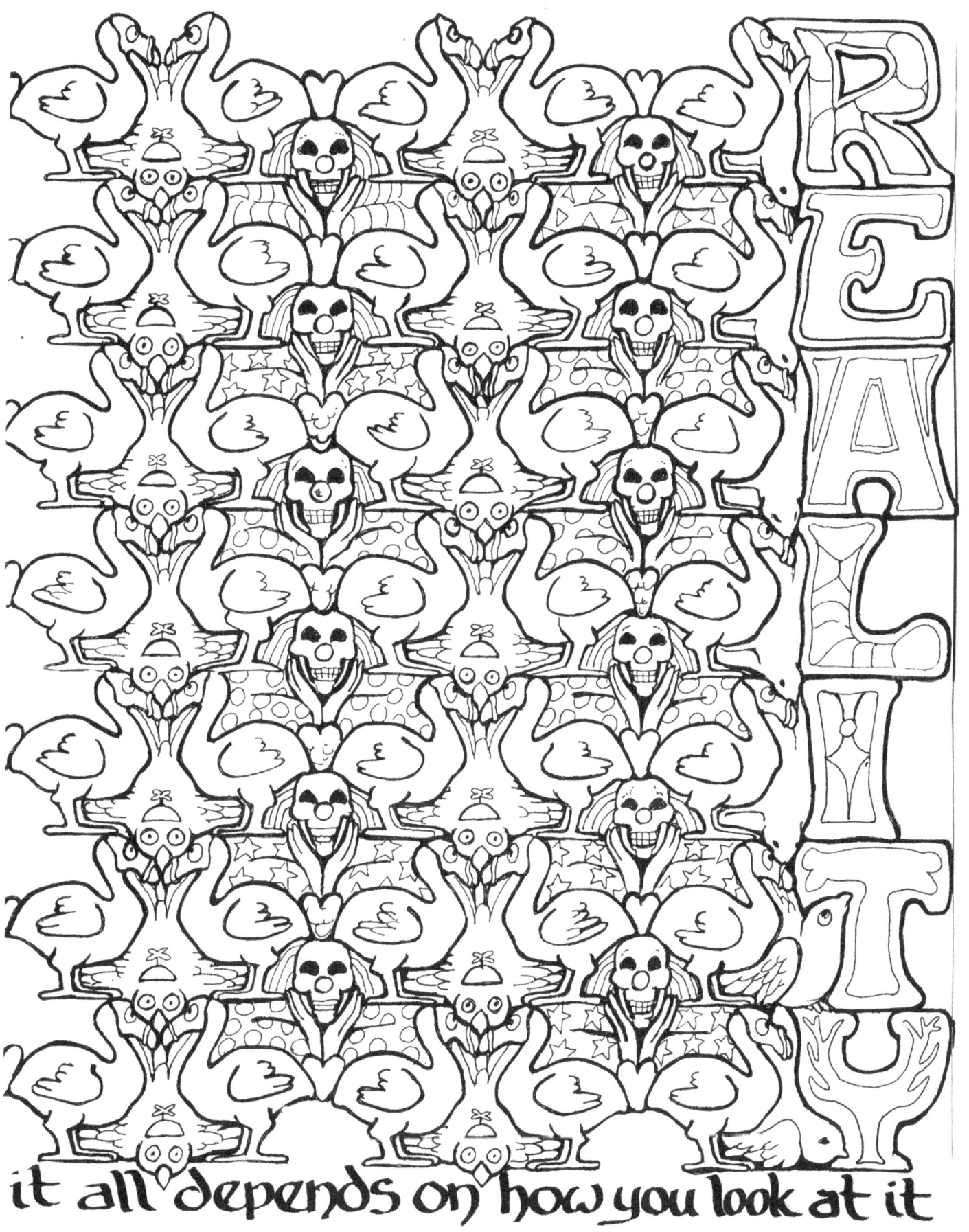

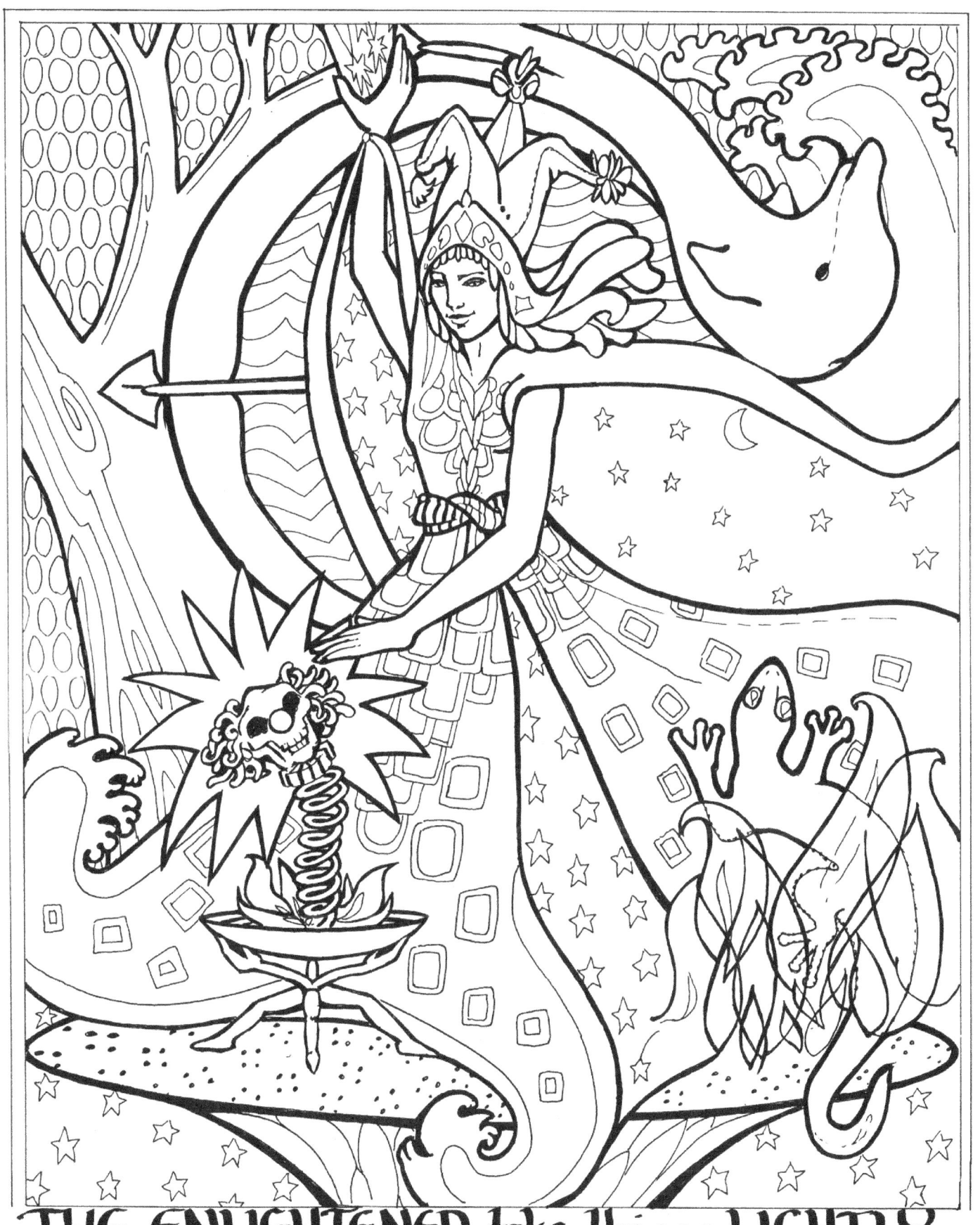

THE ENLIGHTENED take things LIGHTLY

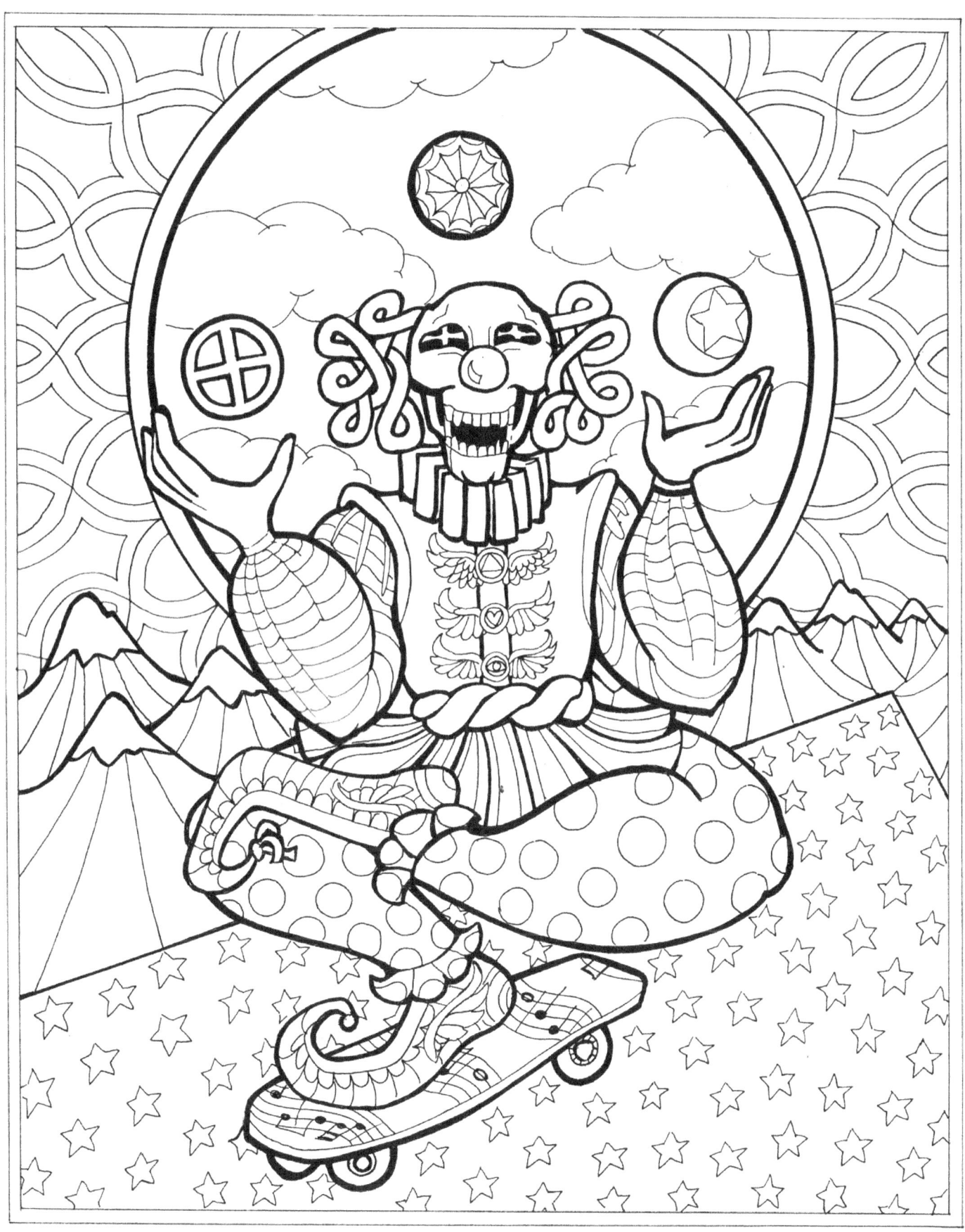

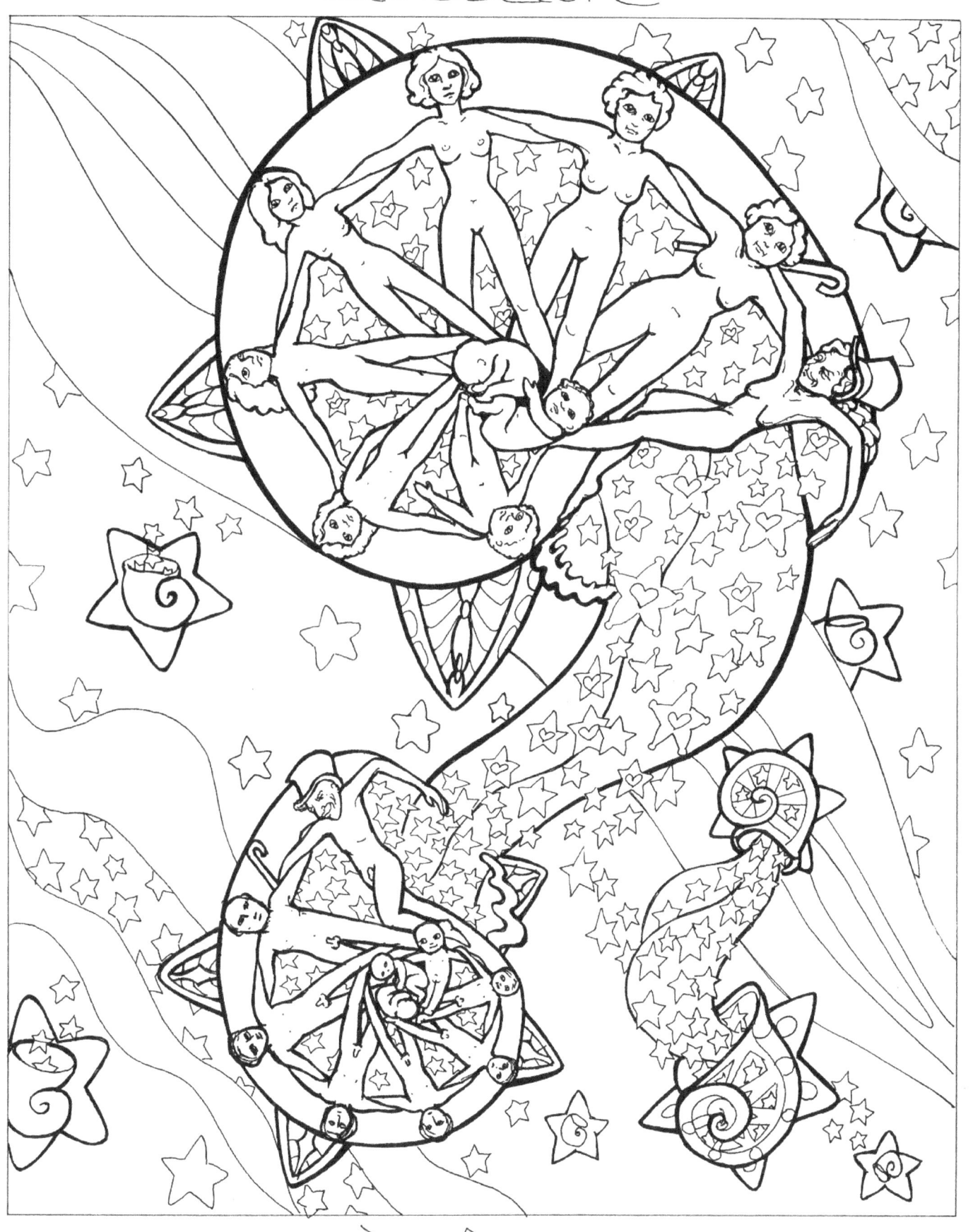

Question

and Answer

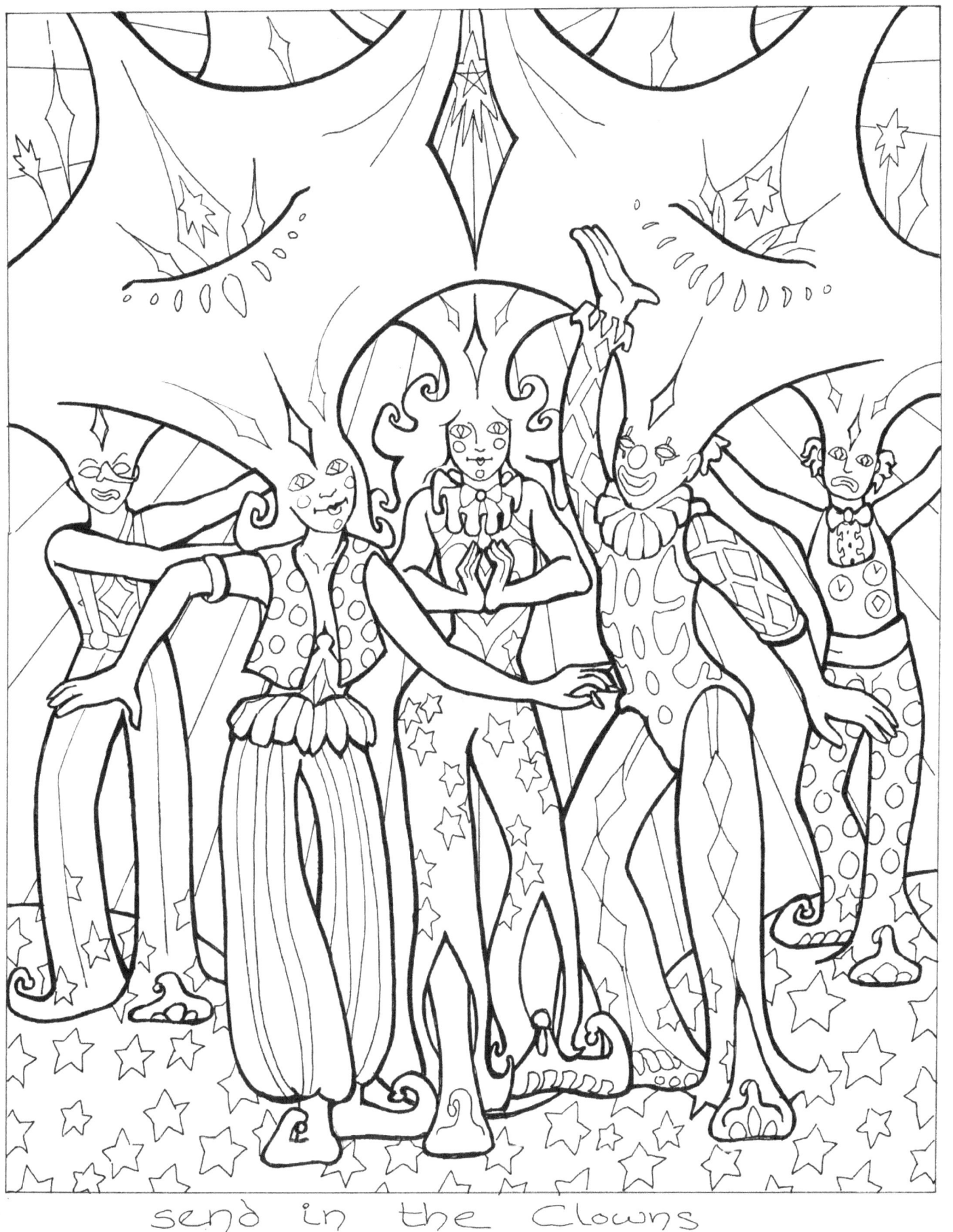
send in the Clowns

no two equals are

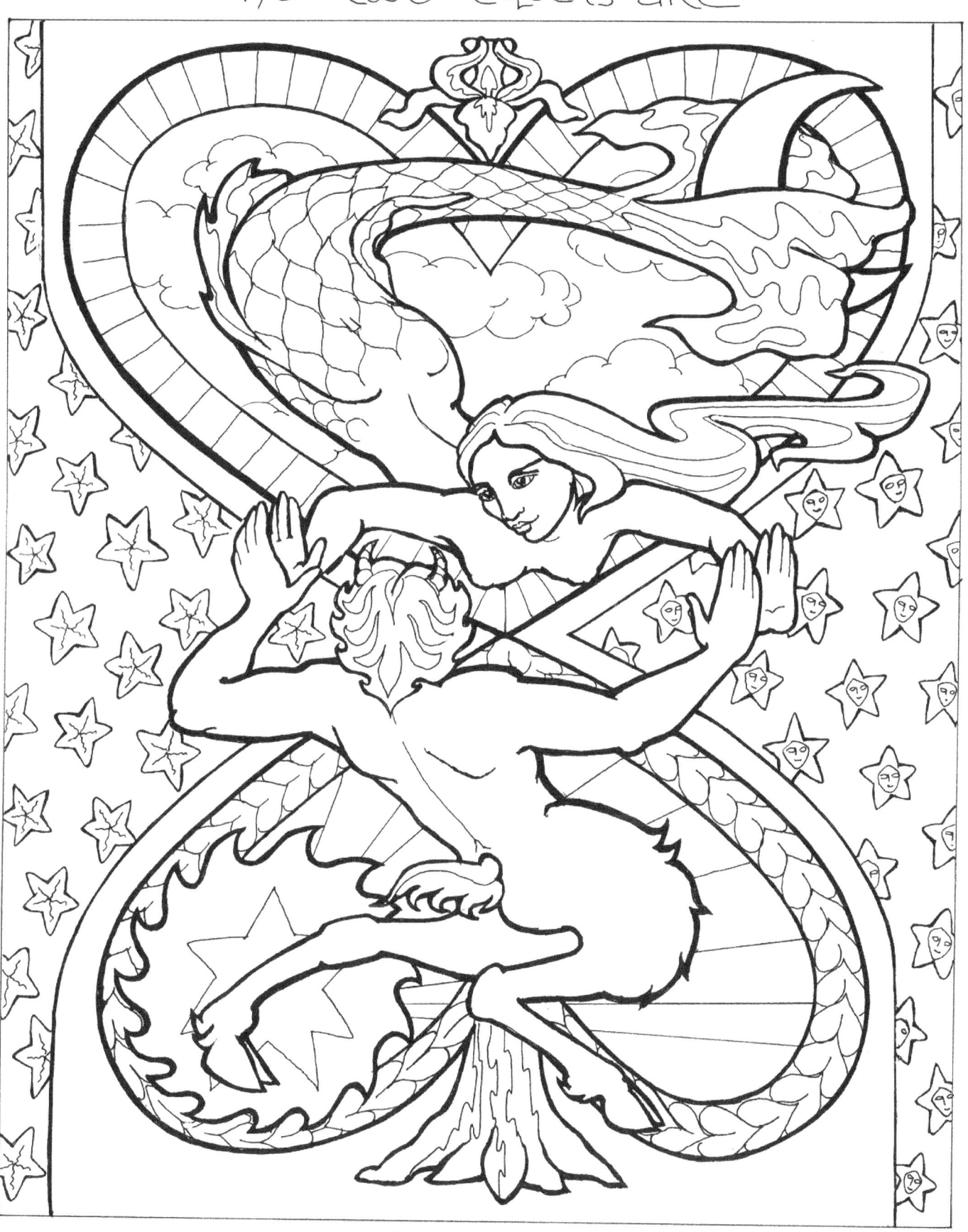

the same

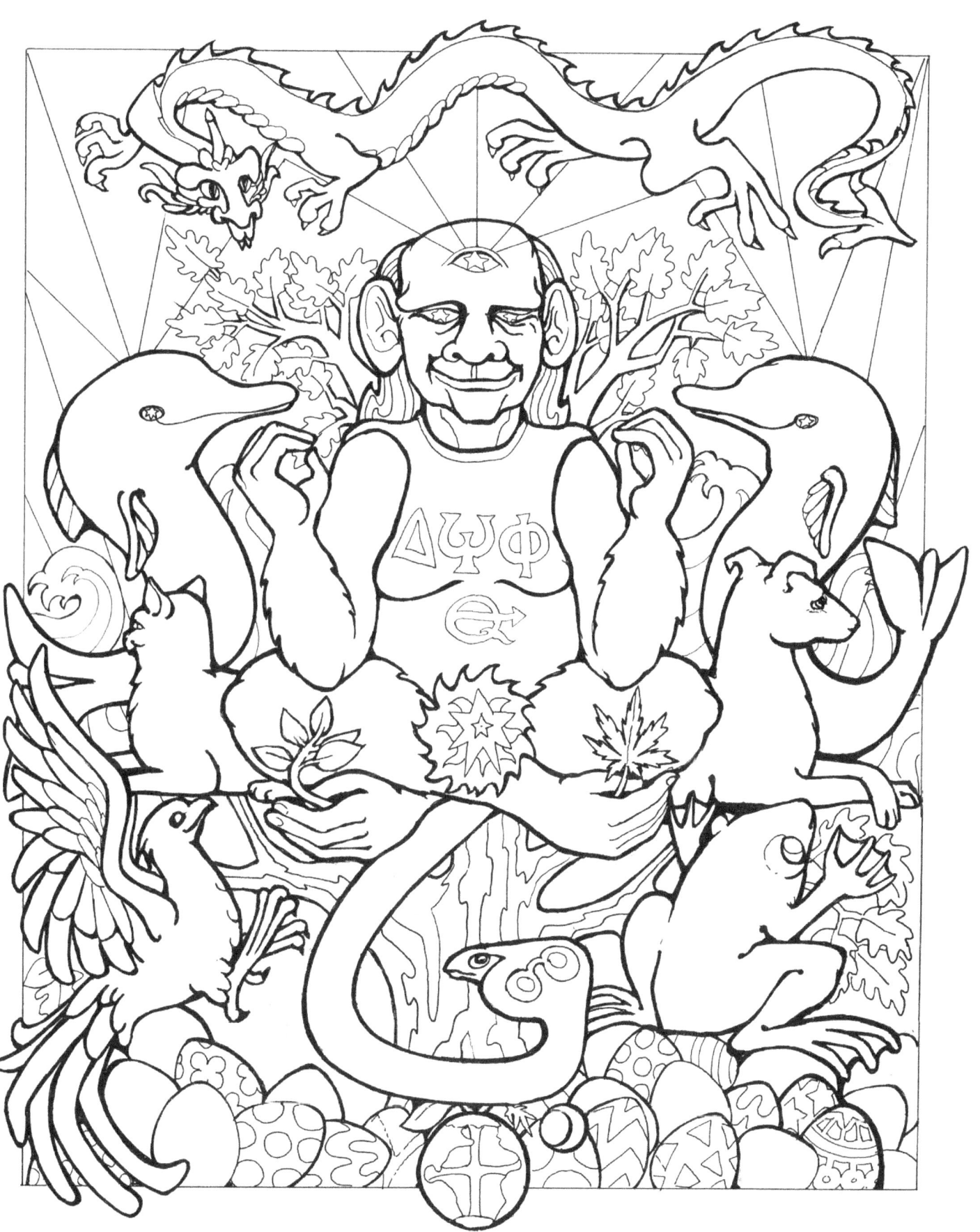

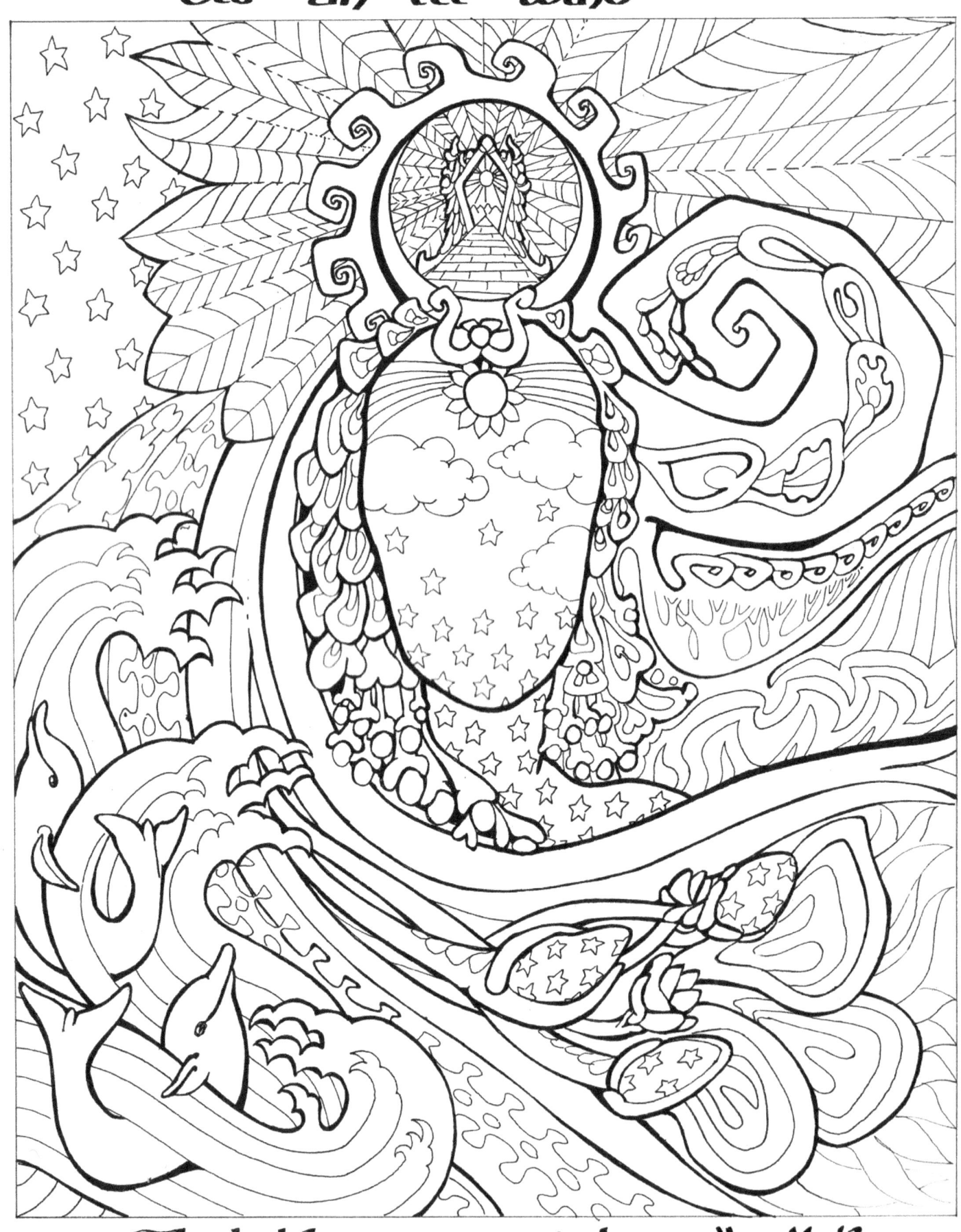

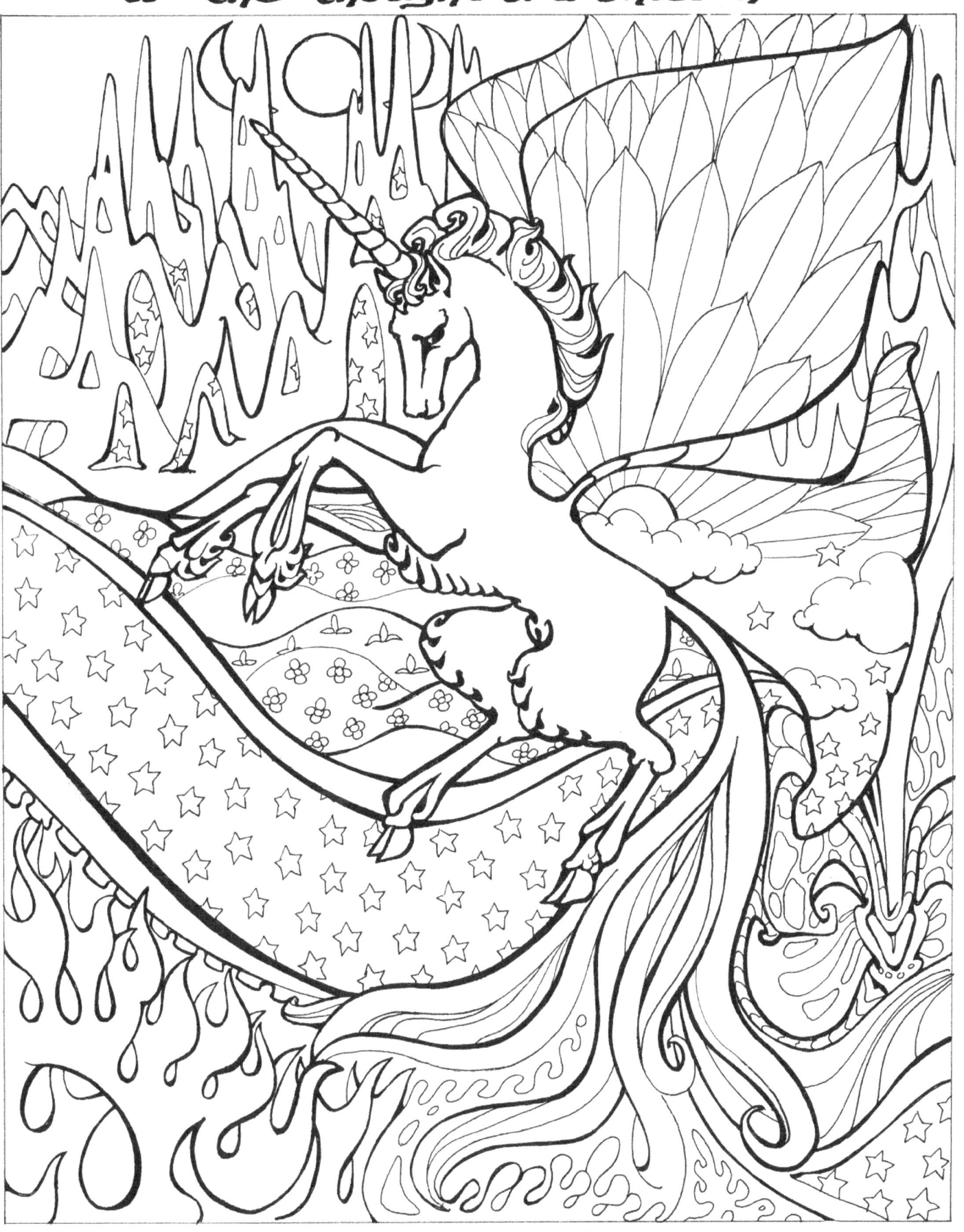

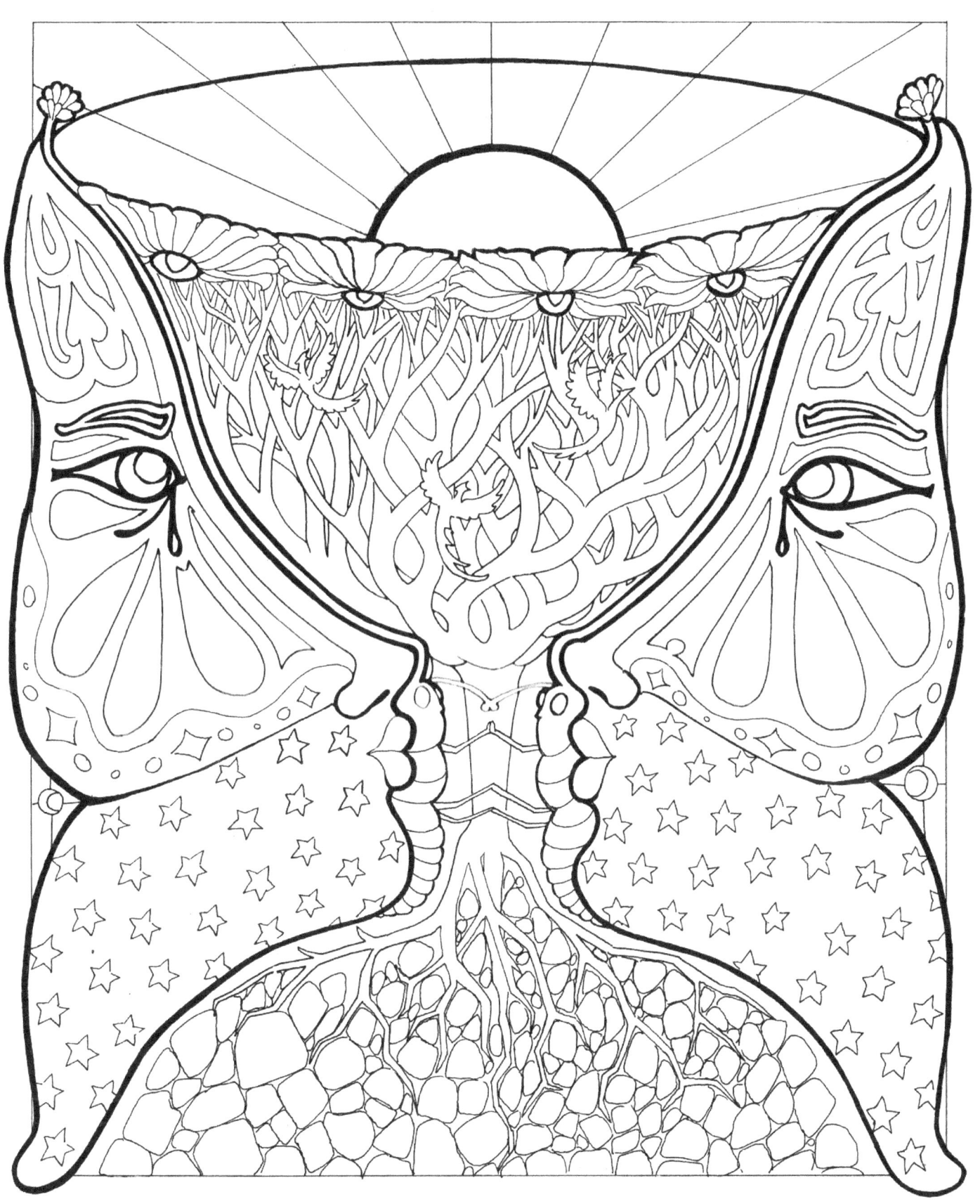

www.ingramcontent.com/pod-product-compliance
Lightning Source LLC
Chambersburg PA
CBHW062341220526
45469CB00008B/2794